BESTEAMS
BUILDING ENGINEERING STUDENT TEAM EFFECTIVENESS AND MANAGEMENT SYSTEMS

A curriculum guide for faculty

Linda C. Schmidt
Janet A. Schmidt
Paige E. Smith
David I. Bigio
Jeanne Bayer Contardo

University of Maryland, College Park

College House Enterprises, LLC
Knoxville, TN

This textbook is intended to provide accurate and authoritative information regarding the various topics covered. It is distributed with the understanding that the publisher is not engaged in providing legal, accounting, engineering, or other professional services. If legal advice or other expertise is required, the services of a recognized professional should be retained.

The manuscript was prepared using Word with 11-point Times New Roman font. Publishing and Printing Inc., Knoxville, TN printed this book from camera-ready copy.

College House Enterprises, LLC.
5713 Glen Cove Drive
Knoxville, TN 37919 U.S.A.
Phone and Fax: (865) 558-6111
Email: jdally@collegehousebooks.com
http://www.collegehousebooks.com

ISBN 0-9723567-4-6

About the Authors

Dr. Linda C. Schmidt: Dr. Schmidt is an Associate Professor in Mechanical Engineering at University of Maryland, College Park. She completed her doctorate in Mechanical Engineering at Carnegie Mellon University and holds B.S. and M.S. degrees from Iowa State University for work in Industrial Engineering, specializing in queuing theory and organization research. At UMCP, she has been active in teaching the junior-level product development course and has co-authored two editions of the course textbook. Dr. Schmidt's interest in research on training for engineering project teams has resulted in the founding of BESTEAMS, a research group for the improvement of training materials for engineering project teams, and presentation of research through ASEE conferences and publications.

Dr. Janet A. Schmidt: Dr. Schmidt is the Assistant Dean for Research and Assessment in the College of Education at the University of Maryland, College Park. She received her Ph.D. from the University of Minnesota in Counseling and Personnel Services. A licensed psychologist, Dr. Schmidt is an assessment specialist with expertise in engineering student learning outcome evaluation. She is a co-PI of the BESTEAMS grant as well as three additional NSF grants related to teamwork in the context of learning and gender. She has served as the Director of Student Research in The Clark School of Engineering, Director of Institutional Studies, and Coordinator of the Maryland Longitudinal Study. Finally, Dr. Schmidt is an Affiliate Assistant Professor in the Counseling and Personnel Services department of the University's College of Education.

Dr. Paige E. Smith: Dr. Smith is the Director of the Women in Engineering program at the University of Maryland, College Park. She earned her doctorate in Industrial and Systems Engineering (ISE) with a focus in Management System Engineering from Virginia Tech. She received her M.S. in ISE and B.S. in Engineering Science and Mechanics from Virginia Tech. Her research interests involve socio-technical systems, with an emphasis on project management and teams, and gender diversity. In her position as Director of the Women in Engineering program, she is responsible for providing leadership to the college for recruiting and retaining women in the field. She is currently the Secretary for the Women in Engineering Programs & Advocates Network (WEPAN).

Dr. David I. Bigio: Dr. Bigio is an Associate Professor in Mechanical Engineering at the University of Maryland, College Park. He completed his doctorate at the Massachusetts Institute of Technology and has spearheaded the redesign of a number of core engineering courses at the University of Maryland, including the Engineering Project, Fluid Dynamics and capstone Engineering Design courses. He was a CTE-Lilly Teaching Fellow for 1996-1997 and received the Kent Poole Senior Faculty Teaching Award for 2002-2003. Further, he has been an active BESTEAMS participant and is a co-PI on the grant, presenting at workshops, developing material, and providing on-going assessment.

Ms. Jeanne Bayer Contardo: Ms. Contardo is the BESTEAMS graduate assistant and is a doctoral student in higher education policy at the University of Maryland, College Park. She earned her M.A. from Teachers College, Columbia University, and her B.A. from the University of Washington. At both locations she taught seminars on learning styles and working together in teams. Her current research interests include systemic change occurring in higher education and higher education finance.

Acknowledgments

Many thanks to all those who have helped with this project but especially to our partners serving as Campus Coordinators at other institutions, who piloted the modules, provided ongoing feedback, and attended workshops to promote and disseminate this important information.

Dr. Clay Gloster, Associate Professor of Engineering at Howard University

Dr. Sarah Mouring, Associate Professor of Naval Architecture and Ocean Engineering at the United States Naval Academy

Dr. Gregory Wilkins, Assistant Professor of Electrical and Computer Engineering at Morgan State University

Contents

Preface vii

Chapter 1   INTRODUCTION.. 1

    1.1   Overview 1
    1.2   The Evolution of BESTEAMS... 2
    1.3   Answering Changing Needs in Engineering Education 3
    1.4   Book Layout 6
    1.5   The Three Domains at the Introductory Level 7
    1.6   Summary 8
    1.7   Sources Cited for Introduction 9

Chapter 2   TEAMWORK 101 11

    2.1   Overview of Preparation 11
    2.2   Assigning students to project teams 11
    2.3   Considerations for Team Grading 14
    2.4   Managing "slackers" or non-contributing team members........... 16
    2.5   Dealing with dysfunctional teams 18
    2.6   Maximizing the team experience for women and other underrepresented groups............. 21
    2.7   Sources Cited 23

Chapter 3   BESTEAMS MODULE PERSONAL KNOWLEDGE 25

    3.1   Introduction to Module.. 25
    3.2   David Kolb's Experiential Learning Model: Theoretical Foundations 25
    3.3   Sources Cited 28
    3.4   50-Minute Class Overview: Understanding Your Learning Style I 30
    3.5   BESTEAMS Module Implementation Plan (MIP) 31
    3.6   Personal Awareness for Students: References 44

Chapter 4   BESTEAMS MODULE INTERPERSONAL EFECTIVENESS 47

    4.1   Introduction to Module.. 47
    4.2   Team Functioning: Theoretical Foundations 47
    4.3   Sources Cited 52
    4.4   50-Minute Class Overview: Working Effectively within Teams 54
    4.5   BESTEAMS Module Implementation Plan (MIP) 55
    4.6   Interpersonal Effectiveness for Students: References 68

Chapter 5   BESTEAMS MODULE PROJECT MANAGEMENT 71

    5.1   Introduction to Module.. 71
    5.2   Theoretical Foundations... 71
    5.3   Sources Cited 76
    5.4   50-Minute Class Overview: Introductory Project Management 78
    5.5   BESTEAMS Module Implementation Plan (MIP) 79
    5.6   Project Management for Students: References 99

Chapter 6   CONCLUSION..**101**

    6.1   BESTEAMS Material..101

    6.2   Best Practices—Using the Modules 102

    6.3   BESTEAMS Success..102

    6.4   The Future of BESTEAMS 103

    6.5   Resources...103

APPENDIX...**105**

INDEX..**113**

Preface

Every engineering instructor who has uttered the following sentence had seen students grimace, roll their eyes, begin gesturing to each other or shrink deep into their seats in horror.

"This course will include a team project worth a significant portion of your grade."

This seems like an odd reaction to the announcement of a team activity. After all, engineering is a team sport. Our engineering programs are ABET accredited only after demonstrating a curriculum that includes teaching our students the ability to function in multidisciplinary teams. The truth is that working in teams is a skill that instructors must teach along with all the other professional abilities we require from our graduates. This book is designed to give engineering instructors the means, methods, and motivation to add team training modules to courses that include team projects.

Our work on developing formal materials for team training grew from the synergy of engineering education initiatives already underway at the University of Maryland, College Park. The *Introduction to Engineering Design* (ENES 100) course was initiated under the auspices of the NSF-sponsored ECSEL coalition in 1990, and its centerpiece was participation in a team-based engineering project. Students actively worked to design, build, and test human items such as powered water pumps, solar desalinators, and postal weighing scales. The deliberate teaching of teamwork was included in the course. The inclusion of team training in ENES 100 was facilitated in part by the enthusiasm of the faculty members involved in ground breaking curriculum development and the fact that the faculty members themselves were taught team training skills as a part of their ESCEL involvement.

We present to you an introductory team training book, supported in part by a Course, Curriculum, and Laboratory Improvement (DUE-CCLI-0089079) grant from the National Science Foundation (*Title: Implementing the BESTEAMS model of team development across the curriculum*). Any opinions, findings, and conclusions or recommendations expressed in this material are those of the author(s) and do not necessarily reflect the views of the National Science Foundation. This text incorporates characteristics designed specifically to enable use by engineering faculty. First, the curriculum is composed of three distinct tracks based on key domains of team functioning (personal knowledge, interpersonal effectiveness, and project management skills). Second, the material is designed in discrete "modules" or individual building blocks that can be combined by engineering faculty in ways that make the most sense for their particular students and team projects. Third, each module includes background material for instructors, presentation outlines, interactive student activities, and suggestions for customizing the material for different class sizes and lengths. Finally, the modules presented here include complete sets of Microsoft PowerPoint® slides that can be downloaded and used "as-is" or customized by instructors. The website for downloading the Training Modules can be found at **http://www.enme.umd.edu/labs/BESTEAMS/**

We are grateful to various individuals for their support of the project since its inception. Prior to NSF funding, the University of Maryland's Mechanical Engineering (ME) department, under the leadership of Professor Dav Anand, increased the number of team based courses in the ME department and encouraged ME faculty members to participate in BESTEAMS training activities—many thanks to those who assisted this effort. In addition, individuals associated with ENES 100 played key roles in the development of the present work. Dr. Thomas Regan, professor of Chemical Engineering and head of the ECSEL project, embraced BESTEAMS training and suggested using advanced undergraduates as team facilitators in ENES 100. More recently Dr. Gary Pertmer, Associate Dean of Education in the Clark School, has continued to endorse and support team training in this introductory class. Other individuals to whom thanks is due include: Dr. George Dieter, Dr. Nariman Farvardin, Dr. Patricia Mead, Dr. Marjorie Erickson-Kirk, Dr. Bob Lent, Dr. Carol Colbeck, Jeannie Brown Leonard, and ASEE, which has supported BESTEAMS dissemination activities by sponsoring workshops at the national annual convention for the past three years (2002, 2003, 2004). Our friend and publisher, Dr. Jim Dally, used his engineering project management skill to motivate us to finish this book on time and under budget. Thanks Jim! Finally, we owe a special thanks to our partners at Howard University, Morgan State, and the United States Naval Academy: Dr. Clay Gloster, Dr. Gregory Wilkins and Dr. Sarah Mouring, respectively. Thanks to their collaboration and encouragement, this project is much richer than anything we could have achieved on our own.

We hope you find this work helpful when facing an audience of students contemplating an engineering team project. We welcome feedback and look forward to hearing how you will use this material to increase student learning and satisfaction.

Linda C. Schmidt
Janet A. Schmidt
Paige E. Smith
David I. Bigio
Jeanne Bayer Contardo

The Clark School of Engineering
University of Maryland, College Park

January, 2005

Chapter 1 INTRODUCTION

1.1 Overview

The announcement in the engineering classroom of a required "team project" has the potential to strike fear into the heart of even the most confident undergraduate. With visions of unequal workload looming, students must be reminded that the project team is a certainty for those in the engineering fields. The Accreditation Board for Engineering and Technology (ABET) published a series of accreditation requirements related to engineering program outcomes for baccalaureate degrees earned that were adopted nationally in 2000. Prominent among these expected outcomes is the "ability to function on multi-disciplinary teams" (ABET 2003).

Beyond accreditation requirements, there are numerous reasons for integrating teamwork experiences into undergraduate classrooms. Unlike many other careers, graduates of engineering programs are typically faced with a work environment that immediately requires teamwork skills. Providing students with opportunities to develop these abilities in the classroom may be directly tied to their post-graduation success and their long-term satisfaction with their undergraduate education.

This text emphasizes teamwork as compared to working in groups. The reasons for this become apparent once the differences between the two are examined. Many students have experienced working in groups, often as a means for completing homework assignments. In group work, each person is responsible for the same deliverable: groups are used to discuss a set of items or problems and share solution strategies. In contrast, teamwork requires more interdependence than group work. The deliverable is a joint project comprised of many separate tasks; completion necessitates each team member participating in varying responsibilities. No two team members will ever have an identical list of duties. The team project itself is the means by which students demonstrate their mastery of the material taught in the course.

From the educational perspective, positive team experiences can motivate students to perform at higher levels. Well-functioning teams have been shown to improve learning and retention in non-engineering fields, especially for members of underrepresented groups (Barra, 1993; Belenky, Clenchy, Goldberger, & Tarule, 1986; Fullilove & Treisman, 1990; Smith & Waller, 1997; Wankat & Oreoviez, 1993). As non-majority students move toward engineering degrees in greater numbers, providing opportunities for them to work with one another helps promote development of sustaining skills and relationships. Lastly, teams are a vital construct in engineering education because they provide a realistic learning environment and a skill proving ground.

However, the creation of successfully operating teams that produce positive learning experiences for all members is not simple and the consequences of poor team interactions can be severe. Individuals in dysfunctional teams may achieve low content mastery and poor comprehension of successful team processes. Students may even question their desire to persist in the field of engineering since teamwork is so ubiquitous (Bigio & Schmidt, 1999). Thus, it is critical that engineering educators determine strategies that will foster positive team experiences and enhance the learning of all students within teams.

Despite the importance of successful team interactions, many engineering faculty members do not know how to teach the necessary components of effective teamwork. As a result, instructors rely on intuition or ad hoc experience and students sink or swim. While instructors may strive to find time for development of new course materials that facilitate positive project teams, pressures to publish, hold office hours, perform original research, serve within the campus community, and teach highly evaluated courses may all take precedence. "Opportunity cost" is the overriding issue preventing curricular reform, as faculty members understandably weigh the time required to develop a new course or learn new pedagogies against their current, and more highly rewarded, commitments (Ferren and Kinch, 2003).

1.2 The Evolution of BESTEAMS

The *Building Engineering Student Team Effectiveness and Management Systems* (BESTEAMS) project developed from a first-hand awareness of the importance of successful student team experiences as well as an understanding of the difficulties experienced by faculty in facilitating such interactions. Supported by an NSF grant (DUE-CCLI-0089079), BESTEAMS' early work included establishing baseline understanding of engineering faculty's opinions and experience in teamwork. Faculty member interviews conducted at four different types of educational environments (a large public urban institution, a historically black college, a US military college and a predominately African American university) revealed commitment to using engineering project teams in the classroom. However, most faculty members reported no formal training in teaching teams how to work well together in order to maximize learning (Mead, 2000). The BESTEAMS project was initiated to meet this challenge by creating a comprehensive teamwork curriculum especially for the engineering classroom. This book describes the first of three levels of the curriculum (Introductory) and is designed to provide engineering instructors a pedagogically sound basis for training students to succeed in project teams.

BESTEAMS was founded in 1997 by a group of female mechanical engineering faculty members at the University of Maryland. These scholars sought to transform the academic and professional engineering environments to be accessible for all engineers...especially women. To encourage positive change, the BESTEAMS project strove to train engineering students to recognize and accept diverse learning, communication, and behavior styles in themselves and in their colleagues, independent of gender. The *team* was selected as the central organizing concept around which to fashion this improved learning environment for the reasons articulated in Section 1.1 above. Implementing the material in this book will heighten students' awareness of differences in learning and communication styles, as well as how these differences can affect team dynamics and productivity. As a result, discussions of diversity can avoid gender or racial stereotypes and increase student understanding of the many approaches human beings employ for accomplishing tasks.

Thanks to multiple sources of funding, the BESTEAMS members at the University of Maryland College Park were able to expand their efforts and formally develop partnerships with Howard University (Washington, DC), Morgan State University (Baltimore, MD), and the United States Naval Academy (Annapolis, MD). These partnerships offered different climates for implementation trials and eventually produced material that was successfully taught to a wide range of engineering instructors and students. Faculty members from these institutions were asked to assess the training in terms of its clarity and usefulness in improving engineering team projects. In addition, faculty from around the nation attending BESTEAMS workshops (including workshops presented during the 2003, 2004, 2005 ASEE national conventions; 2002, 2003 The Lilly Scholars conference; 2002 FIE conference; and 2002, 2004 NCIIA national conferences) have contributed to the refinement of the materials. Finally, engineering students themselves have evaluated the modules over this same three year time period. Their feedback has been incorporated into the materials presented in this faculty guide. Such expansive testing has demonstrated the wide adaptability of the BESTEAMS team training model.

The BESTEAMS team training philosophy stresses the following:

- Teams are more than collections of individuals. Six well-meaning undergraduates can form one dysfunctional team deficient in task productivity and engineering subject mastery. Faculty must consider both individual and team performance.

- Team interactions are both one-on-one and one-on-many. In other words, teams require interpersonal expertise that includes skills in dyadic communication as well as group interaction and management.

- Team performance is complex. Explicit training in how teams can maximize their effectiveness in terms of group process and achieving team objectives, including the mastery of engineering content, is critical.

1.3 Answering Changing Needs in Engineering Education

Traditionally, engineering faculty members taught technical material by focusing on basic science competence and the engineering product or system to be developed. Additional abilities, such as interpersonal communication skills, were expected to arise from other sources. However, due to changes in industry and the expectations of accreditation sources (e.g., ABET EAC 2003), as well as increased focus on multidisciplinary-based problems, today's faculty members are faced with teaching future engineers additional non-technical skills, including effective teamwork.

Non-technical skills are sometimes referred to as "professional" or "soft" skills. The term professional skills is favored since soft appears to connote a lack of rigor or importance of the material. While external audiences such as employers and ABET are clear regarding the need for professional skills training in engineering education, engineering faculty and students have been slow to respond. As noted above, faculty members' reluctance may be due to their own lack of training in these skills and emersion in the higher education environment where teamwork has not been strongly rewarded. Likewise, anecdotal observation and some research has suggested that engineering students often come to the field because they like science and problem solving, not because they excel at working with people (Felder, 2002). Thanks to these environmental characteristics, a situation has developed where talented instructors and students alike need encouragement as well as additional tools in order to explore new methods of teaching and learning related to professional skill development.

Smith and Waller (1997) have investigated the current engineering terrain and identified changes in the way education for engineering professionals is viewed. They suggest that because expectations for how engineers function are changing, methods for teaching and sharing knowledge must also adapt (see table 1.1).

Table 1.1 Learning Attributes

	Old Standard		**New Ideal**
Knowledge	One way: transmitted from faculty to students	→	Two way: jointly assembled by students and faculty
Students	Empty receptacle to be filled by expert instructor	→	Active learner, explorer, and shaper of knowledge
Method of learning	Rote memorization	→	Create relationships and integrations
Faculty intent	Serve to categorize students and size up abilities	→	Facilitate development of competencies and talents
Climate	Adaptation of dominant culture/uniformity	→	Appreciation of diversity and nurturing of personal esteem
Teaching premise	Any knowledgeable individual can teach	→	Teaching is complicated and requires extensive training

Adapted from Smith, 2000

Designing, supervising, and evaluating student project teams to ensure successful team process as well as team outcome is challenging for many engineering faculty members. Of these responsibilities, engineering instructors generally feel most comfortable evaluating team *products*. They have been trained in design, production issues and constraints, and can judge the feasibility of alternative engineering solutions or processes. Therefore, as a result of faculty training and experience, student team projects are often over-evaluated in terms of emphasis on engineering products and under-evaluated in terms of team processes.

The material provided here is a resource for those faculty members who wish to introduce their students to methods which encourage effective team processes. The complete BESTEAMS curriculum is designed to take students through introductory, intermediate, and advanced training in the form of discrete, independent modules that can be introduced in a variety of ways into existing engineering classes (see table 1.2). In its simplest form, a module is a complete lesson plan. Modules are designed to fit within one class session and can stand on their own or be used as part of a longer, more extensive training experience. Ideally, professors within a department will coordinate their efforts to ensure that students receive exposure to all of the modules during their undergraduate work. By the time students complete the advanced team training modules, they should feel comfortable and confident regarding three key areas of team functioning as defined by BESTEAMS: Personal Knowledge, Interpersonal Effectiveness, and Project Management.

The first domain critical to successful teaming is Personal Knowledge. Individuals must be self-aware in order to bring their strengths to the team. Similarly, if a team is to perform at a maximum level, participants must contribute their best talents to the joint effort. Knowing what one does well and appreciating the fact that others on the team bring different talents to the table are key learning outcomes in this domain. The Personal Knowledge track is composed of modules in three levels. The Introductory module focuses on understanding learning style preferences using the Kolb Learning Style Inventory (Kolb, 1999); the Intermediate module expands upon this material by introducing the Felder Learning Styles Inventory (Felder & Solomon, n.d.) designed specifically for engineering students; and the Advanced module finishes with a unit on different styles of team leadership.

The second domain focuses on Interpersonal Effectiveness: namely, how to manage team interactions, including conflicts and decision making, and methods for using that knowledge to create a smoothly functioning team experience. This domain includes training materials related to what most consider team dynamics. The Introductory Interpersonal Effectiveness module presents basic communication skills, including giving and receiving feedback, and different types of brainstorming techniques for idea generation. In the Intermediate level of the curriculum, students learn conflict resolution techniques. Students conclude with the Advanced module where they are taught negotiation skills and perspectives.

The third domain included in the BESTEAMS curriculum model is Project Management. This domain is especially important to team performance in an engineering context. Engineering projects, unlike many other disciplines, are extremely complex and involve multiple sub-projects and assignments, each with their own deadlines and interdependencies for completion. The goal of the Project Management track is to teach students a number of tools that will help them successfully schedule the various components of their team project. In the Introductory module, students are exposed to the need for specific project management skills and ways to break a project into manageable units that aid task completion. Later, the Intermediate materials address project tracking and the more complicated scoping processes. Finally, in the Advanced module students are taught how to close out a team project successfully and bring closure to the team participants.

In sum, the BESTEAMS curriculum is designed to be both developmental, moving from simple to more advanced material, and comprehensive, including three different domains of effective engineering team practice. This particular text provides instructors with the Introductory material needed to initiate the notion of team training as a legitimate engineering endeavor and the course material related to the three domains. For information on the Intermediate and Advanced modules, please visit the BESTEAMS website at:
http://www.enme.umd.edu/labs/BESTEAMS/

Table 1.2 Module Overview

Tracks	Personal Knowledge	Interpersonal Effectiveness	Project Management
Introductory	Kolb Learning Styles	Team Development & Communications Basics	Managing Your Project: Planning & Time
Intermediate	Felder Learning Styles	Conflict Resolution	Project Scope Planning & Performance Tracking
Advanced	Leadership & Teams	Team Conflict & Negotiation	Project Closure & Keys to Project Power

1.4 Book Layout

Before presenting the Introductory modules, a review of basic information on team structure and management of typical team problems is in order. As previously discussed, while many faculty members have experience in teaching team based classes, their approaches may be the result of trial and error rather than pedagogically sound practice. Chapter 2 provides information on many frequently asked questions raised when setting up project teams. Topics include assigning students to project teams, considerations for team grading, managing "slackers" or non-contributing team members, dealing with dysfunctional teams, and maximizing the experience of women and other underrepresented groups on teams. Further resources on this subject are listed at the end of the chapter.

Following this overview of team basics, chapters 3, 4, and 5 present the Introductory modules for each of the three domains. Each chapter follows a specific structure designed to allow engineering instructors to flexibly implement the material depending on student need and project requirements. In sequential order, these components are:

A) An introduction to the module and an explanation of background theory on which the module training is based;
B) A module overview for quick reference, including student learning objectives;
C) The Module Implementation Plan (MIP), which provides step-by-step instructions for presenting the material as well as a hard copy of the PowerPoint® slides designed to accompany the lesson; and
D) References for further exploration of the subject matter.

Within each module, there are two options available for the class session. Instructor choice should depend on the length of time available for team training, the degree of students' previous experience, and the level of competence desired.

- The 50-minute lesson plan provides a firm foundation in the subject and can be taught in a typical class period. Through a combination of lecture and group activity, students learn why the domain is vital to team functioning, and how to use the information learned in future team experiences.

- An extended lesson plan that offers 40 additional minutes of material provides further opportunity for students to practice the material. This lengthier material might be used during a lab or recitation session. Alternatively, some of the material added to the 90 minute sessions can be delivered to the students in the form of homework or other out-of-class assignments.

Each MIP provides teaching strategies for both options, so instructors may select which activities are most appropriate for their students. BESTEAMS recognizes that individual classes have their own characteristics; subsequently, activities will hold varying levels of appeal for students.

The MIPs are designed in a layered fashion, which means the instructor may first skim to gain an overview of the material and how it can be taught, and then progress to detailed explanations and instructions. For example, follow-up sections include: a discussion of the ways in which the MIP answers the needs of diverse learners in the classroom, a topic that may be particularly useful for those instructors who are unfamiliar with adapting educational material to different

> Takeaway points are designated by a ✐ symbol for easy identification of the learning goals

learning styles and preferences; class adaptation strategies that will allow further tailoring of the lesson to students' needs, depending on class size, class subject, and the classroom culture; and follow-up resources, including assessment options, and further opportunities to help students master the material through homework assignments and other classroom activities.

Finally, each MIP provides the instructor with pre-designed PowerPoint® slides that can be used in delivering the material. These slides were developed so instructors could avoid time-consuming curriculum development, as well as to provide a point of departure from which adaptation or modification could easily occur. The BESTEAMS PowerPoint® presentations are available for download from our website at:
http://www.enme.umd.edu/labs/BESTEAMS/

1.5 The Three Domains at the Introductory Level

BESTEAMS members have worked to ensure that all material included in the modules was chosen for applicability and efficiency. The following discussion of the rationale behind the subjects covered in each of the Introductory domains demonstrates this effort.

Personal Knowledge

Psychological literature provides many empirically derived theories that can be used to learn about individuals and their differences (Jung, 1990; Kolb, 1983). For the less informed, stereotypes can also function as personal theories through which individuals make judgments about others. Psychologists have speculated that the human need to group or organize perceptions is related to efficiency and conservation: fewer categories are easier to understand (Piaget, 1929). In the case of people, however, stereotyping often results in an important loss of information, when characteristics of the individual are absorbed into the group view. In the case of non-majority team members such as women and racial/ethnic minorities, stereotypes can provide negative lenses with which to interpret behavior. With this in mind, BESTEAMS' material in the Personal Knowledge domain is designed to help students develop a positive "filter" that will teach them about individual differences in an educationally useful manner. Based on our exploration of psychological theories appropriate to engineering education, BESTEAMS chose to use Kolb's Learning Styles as the foundation for this module. The goal is to increase students' self-awareness and understanding of their strengths and weaknesses in the context of the college learning environment. Since this module is often incorporated in the first year or even the first semester of engineering education, most students are receptive to better understanding their learning preferences and how their style compares to those of other engineering students.

This material assists students in identifying their personal learning style and how it impacts their behavior and learning in a team setting. Students also explore the ways in which this information may affect team dynamics and why this knowledge is important. For example, team members often exhibit different preferences; as a result, they will not interpret the task assignment in the same manner. Awareness of this fact may serve to reduce unnecessary friction within the team. By the end of the module, students should be able to anticipate how learning style differences can impact future team interactions.

Interpersonal Effectiveness

The most dreaded aspect of student project teams for many instructors is handling team conflict. Positive team dynamics or interpersonal relationships can make the team experience productive both in terms of delivering the desired project outcome as well as mastery of the class engineering content.

In contrast, poor team interactions can sabotage both of these goals and require much instructor effort to rectify them. Fortunately, the ways that interpersonal dynamics in teams can go astray are well known and with training and awareness can be minimized. This module includes lessons in giving and receiving feedback as well as exercises to improve listening skills. A focus on proactive behavior teaches students to anticipate teammate differences and to view such "not like me" ideas and behavior as opportunities to learn rather than problems to solve. Finally, students are introduced to the stages of team development: forming, storming, norming, performing, and adjourning. It is reassuring to students and instructors alike to know that group conflict (storming) is a normal part of virtually every team experience.

Project Management

As noted above, training in effective teams within the context of engineering must include a recognition that the team tasks are notably more complex and interdependent than projects that occur in other environments. Yet most team projects in the undergraduate curriculum are completed without any training in project management tools and techniques. Indeed, most college students think and manage their academic work within a time horizon of one to two weeks, a time frame much too small for efficient progress on a semester-long engineering project. Beginning in the first year of the BESTEAMS curriculum, students complete a module on project management basics, which includes creating a Gantt chart and supplemental material on the principles of personal time management. In part because they are easy to understand and master, Gantt charts are useful in identifying key tasks and timeline issues related to project completion. The object of this module is to provide basic vocabulary and a fundamental planning tool which enables learners to begin the process of effectively managing a complex, multi-part engineering team assignment.

1.6 Summary

For six years, the BESTEAMS faculty and partners have developed, piloted, revised, and assessed this material and its usefulness for the engineering classroom. As a result, we have uncovered a number of key understandings that help set the context for this book.

- Training in team skills is important. While some teams can function successfully without training, the rule of the Pareto Principle often applies: 80 percent of the instructor's time can go to 20 percent of the class—the problem team. Training in effective teamwork lowers the likelihood that the instructor will have to spend significant time mediating conflicts and can instead facilitate successful projects that maximize student learning.

- Students will believe team training is important if the instructor does. While some may say that team process skills are common sense, research and practice clearly indicates that training in team skills enhances performance (Mead et al., 1999; Parsons et al., 2002). Faculty members that conduct team training in their classes and encourage students to learn such skills in other contexts such as extracurricular activities send a message that the training is worth the effort.

- If team skills and teamwork are to be valued by students, they must be graded. It is a fact that students have many commitments, all of which compete for their time. If an instructor says that effective teamwork is important, but only grades team *products*, a mixed message about the value of professional skills is being sent. Students look to what the instructor grades as the most important course requirements.

- Engineers can master the material presented here even if it takes them out of their comfort zone. It is our intention to provide enough detailed information and structure so that instructors can spend minimum time preparing and researching primary source information on teamwork. Instead, faculty time can be spent adapting and using the information in the classroom as well as having students practice the skills.

- Like all new skills, practice makes perfect. The first time an instructor introduces team training into the classroom may feel awkward. With practice, instructors will be able to teach, evaluate, and use the team training materials provided here with the same aplomb that they teach engineering content.

1.7 Sources Cited for Introduction

ABET. (2003). *Criteria for accrediting engineering programs: Effective for evaluations during the 2003-2004 accreditation cycle.* Retrieved October 8, 2003, from http://www.abet.org/images/Criteria/E1%2003-04%20EAC%20Criteria%2011-15-02.pdf

Barra, R. (1993). *Tips and techniques for team effectiveness.* New Oxford, PA: Barra International.

Belenky, M., Clenchy, G., Goldberger, N.R., & Tarule, J. (1986). *Women's ways of knowing: The development of self, voice, and mind.* New York: Basic Books.

Bigio, D., & Schmidt, J. (1999). Workshop for faculty development based on the underlying pedagogical issues of ABET EC 2000. *Proceedings - Frontiers in Education Conference, 1,* 12a1-5 -12a1-9.

Felder, R.M., Felder, G.N., & Dietz, E.J. (2002). The effects of personality type on engineering student performance and attitudes. *Journal of Engineering Education, 91*(1), 3-17.

Felder, R. M., & Solomon, B.A. (n.d.). Index of Learning Styles Questionaire. Retrieved February 10, 2004 from http://www.engr.ncsu.edu/learningstyles/ilsweb.html

Ferren, A.S., & Kinch, A. (Summer, 2003). The dollars and sense behind general education reform. *Peer Review, 5(4).* Posted to *Tomorrow's Professor* (SM) electronic mailing list on September 24, 2003.

Fullilove, R., & Treisman, P.U. (1990). Mathematics achievement among African American undergraduates at the University of California at Berkeley: An evaluation of the math workshop program. *Journal of Negro Education, 59*(3), 463-478.

Jung, C.G. (1990). *The undiscovered self.* New Jersey: Princeton University Press.

Kolb, D.A. (1983). *Experiential learning: Experience as the source of learning and development.* Prentice Hall, PTR.

Kolb, D.A. (1999). *The Kolb learning style inventory (ver. 3).* Boston: Hay Group.

Mead, P.F., Moore, D., Natishan, M., Schmidt, L., Goswami, I., Brown, S., et al. (1999). Faculty and student views on engineering student team effectiveness. *Journal of Women and Minorities in Science and Engineering, 5(4)*, 351-362.

Parsons, J.R., Seat, J.E., Bennet, R.M., Forrester, J.H., Gilliam, Fred T., Klukken, P.G., et al. (2002). The engage program: Implementing and assessing a new first year experience at the University of Tennessee. *Journal of Engineering Education, 91*(4), 441-446.

Piaget, J. (1929). *The child's conception of the world.* Bruce Javanovich (Trans.). New York: Harcourt.

Smith, K.A., & Waller, A.A. (1997). *New paradigms for engineering education.* Pittsburgh, PA: ASEE/IEEE Frontiers in Education Conference Proceedings.

Smith, K.A. (2000). *Project management and teamwork.* New York: McGraw-Hill.

Wankat, P., & Oreoviez, F. (1993). *Teaching engineering.* New York: McGraw-Hill.

Chapter 2   TEAMWORK 101

2.1 Overview of Preparation

Unlike the corporate team model that strives for or relies upon timely and cost effective development of outstanding products, a primary goal of engineering educators is to facilitate the learning of each student project team member. As previously noted, engineering project teams have the potential to influence the student's satisfaction, sense of competence, and persistence in the field. An "ideal" team experience in engineering education has the following characteristics:

- Positive team performance in terms of both team processes and team outcomes
- Demonstrated student learning of engineering content and skills
- Enhancement of student commitment to engineering as a field, evidenced by increased self confidence, satisfaction, and desire to persist in the engineering curriculum

Instructors recognize the value of studying the best practices of successful student team management. Thus, before presenting the BESETAMS team training modules we offer this collection of suggestions on issues related to the basic set-up and structure of setting up student project teams in order to promote positive team performance. This material includes:

- Assigning students to project teams
- Considerations for team grading
- Managing "slackers" or non-contributing team members
- Tips for dealing with dysfunctional teams
- Maximizing the team experience for women and other underrepresented groups

Each section within this chapter has three parts. The first component introduces the issue, the second segment presents pre-emptive steps that could be taken to avoid the problem, and the third part explains ways for dealing with the situation in the moment. Taken together, the application of collected best practices in teaming and BESTEAMS training materials will facilitate smooth classroom experiences for both instructors and students.

2.2 Assigning students to project teams

One of the most important steps in successful team functioning is careful team formation. Much of what engineering faculty dread about group projects can be traced to ineffectively functioning teams. Subsequently, paying attention to initial team set up can save enormous time and energy later by preventing poor group dynamics and team performance. General considerations regarding team formation include:

Characteristics of the team project: What characteristics among team members will be needed to successfully complete the task? In other words, what skills, abilities, and experiences will be needed by the various team members to complete the required project? If the instructor can determine these factors prior to the start of the project, selection of team members can be balanced so that teams have as many of the needed skills as possible.

Level of experience of students with teamwork: Upper-level students generally have more experience with teams and may know their peers. As a result, less structure from the instructor may be required when assigning students to teams. However, lower-level students may not know other students and their abilities well or realize the importance of a diversity of skills on the team. Therefore, increased faculty assistance with team assignments may be more appropriate with younger students.

Individual differences: Depending on the demographics of the class, few minorities or women students may be available to be assigned to teams. Strategies for the success of women and minorities on student project teams will be the focus of its own section below. In addition, an often overlooked population is non-native English speaking students. This group often struggles to be heard in the dominant culture team experience, and sometimes needs special assistance with writing.

Heading off the issue: Pre-emptive steps

Having decided to intervene in the natural selection process which would allow students to choose their own team members, the instructor may employ the following strategies to create engineering project teams:

Use a Skills Inventory approach: Here the instructor develops a short survey to obtain information about the students before assigning them to their teams. The information collected may be about previous educational and team experiences, such as questions related to key roles the student has played on other teams and specific skills related to the class project, as well as information about logistics, such as when the students are available to meet with the rest of the group and who has a car to pick up supplies. Some instructors also use the survey to ask students if there are any individuals in the class with whom they prefer not to work. See Appendix for a sample Application for Team Membership.

GPA groupings: Another strategy employed by instructors is to group students into teams based on similar GPAs, either cumulative or in selected classes. This option addresses the complaint that smarter students get saddled with all the work or are held back by their less talented co-workers in teams where members' grades are more heterogeneous. This can be an interesting strategy because teamwork and successful projects generally require a range of skills and abilities, only some of which may be related to academic performance. Lower GPA based teams may in fact develop better products or be more smoothly functioning.

Secret ballot: In this team formation strategy, students vote for others with whom they wish to work. Only appropriate with classes where students have some idea who their peers are, secret ballot can be organized so that students build their ideal team by identifying members from the class as well as a rationale for their selection. The ballots are secret in that they are given to the instructor who uses the information to form teams (and who also learns a lot about potential issues of group dynamics, such as perceived slackers or those who have difficult personalities).

Football draft: In this scenario, students describe to the class their previous team experiences and what skills they would contribute to the project team. Based on the oral presentations, each student puts together an "ideal" team based on their peers' qualifications. The instructor reviews the ideal team selections and makes any necessary adjustments (e.g., each student can only participate on one team or ensuring that at least one person on a team has a car if transportation is an issue). A side benefit of this approach is an early assessment of the students' communication and presentation skills.

Resume selection: Here students write resumes where they outline their relevant experiences and strengths with regard to the project. The instructor groups individuals into teams based on the obtained information. Side benefits of this approach are an early indication of writing proficiency and level of skill students have in the project and team arenas. Instructors can assist the process by providing a few examples of student team resumes from previous classes.

Random assignment: Done more often than many faculty members would like to admit, many educators simply assign students at random to small team project groups. Feeling that in the real world people often can not choose their own teammates, random assignment prepares students for later employment. Some faculty members initially group students randomly, but may shift individuals depending on the racial/gender breakdowns that have occurred. Pragmatists will sometimes consider factors such as making sure that each group contains a member with an automobile and that all group members are actually able to meet with each other (e.g., that a common meeting time is possible). While this strategy requires less work on the part of the instructor initially, experience has shown that this approach often results in problems during the course of the project. It is our belief that instructors should structure the team experience for learning as carefully as they would prepare a lecture.

Strategic team member assignment: Try including at least two members of the non-majority group on each team, especially with younger, less experienced students. If a skills inventory approach is taken for team assignments, include a question about team preferences (e.g., would you prefer assignment to a team that includes another student of the same race or gender?). With upper level students, placing one female or minority on a team may provide them a more realistic work experience. However, it is important to monitor the team to ensure that these individuals are being included in all team activities and are not marginalized. Finally, instructors themselves should not be afraid to ask students how their experience with the team is going and to intervene when necessary.

In the moment: Dealing with the issue in real time

What if, despite the instructor's best efforts in making assignments, students come forward with complaints about their teammates? What can be done?

Work directly with the entire team: This is the teachable moment. Students have the opportunity to learn conflict management skills that separate the simple technicians from the skilled manager. Review the steps of conflict management and good communication skills from the BESTEAMS interpersonal module. For example, has feedback been given to the problematic team members? Have the expectations for the team roles and deliverables been clarified? Are there extenuating circumstances that might warrant an instructor intervention? Help the students draw up a plan that involves them in the solution.

Speak with the "problem" student(s): If student interventions are ineffective, speaking directly to the identified problem student is the next step. Taking a consultant stance may help with this interaction. What is the student's point of view on the interactions? Does the student see the same problem as the others? Sometimes instructors make the mistake of believing the team, only to find out there is more to the story.

Change team assignments: Depending on the nature of the problem, and the students involved, some instructors change team assignments or go back to team selection strategies to re-align student teams. Some instructors finalize teams only after a few weeks when students have had a chance to get to know each other, and ideally after a mini-project of some sort has been accomplished by the group. The success of the mini-project may suggest how the team is likely to work on future projects. If there are more than minor issues among the team members, as reflected in peer and team assessments, the instructor might consider shifting some students to different teams. Moving several students at the same time makes the transition less traumatic for everyone.

2.3 Considerations for Team Grading

There are four primary issues of concern for instructors who grade engineering team projects. First is how to balance the grading of individual student performance and that of the team. In other words, should all students on the team receive the same grade and should this grade be equal to the team grade or a combination of individual effort and team work?

The second issue is how to incorporate peer evaluations into the team and individual grades. If an instructor decides that peer data should be included, the question becomes how to ensure that the peer data are valid and therefore usable.

Third, some instructors struggle with the degree to reward successful projects versus effort. In other words, what percentage of the student's grade should be determined by the success of the final project, and how much by the performance of the team and its process? A terribly functioning team can produce a successful engineering project, as well as the reverse. Instructors must be clear about their goals for the class with regard to outcome (final engineering project) and process (team functioning).

Finally, instructors must consider individual mastery of engineering content and grading in a team context. In the team situation, students often gravitate toward preferred roles or tasks. For example, if a student is especially competent in CAD drawings, she might choose or be pressured by the team to assume that role in the team project. By repeatedly specializing in one area, students may be shortchanging their education in the broad subject matter of the project. Therefore, instructors need to consider the degree of content mastery they expect from each of the team members and how they will assess that competency.

Heading off the issue: Pre-emptive steps

Communicate expectations: Many instructors use a combination of methods to grade team and individual performance. Individual grades may be based on a percentage of individual work (such as on selected exams or quizzes, written reports, or presentations) and peer evaluations. The team grade may be determined by a number of factors such as meeting customer expectations, superior performance, and creativity. In all cases, the methods used to grade the students should be clearly specified in the syllabus.

Peer evaluations: This method can offer the instructor significant insight into team dynamics, if properly employed. Students must be taught how to use peer evaluations in order to be effective. Professors should introduce the importance of peer feedback from the standpoint of future professional practice. Specifics of giving both positive and negative feedback can be taught to students using the Introductory Interpersonal Knowledge module so they have more confidence in their observations. Finally, instructors should ask students to evaluate each other at least several times during the semester: first after an early project deadline, at the midpoint of the class, and certainly at the end. In the initial evaluations, it is helpful to establish that the peer evaluations are not for grading. Instead they present a non-punitive way to identify areas of growth for the team members, and subsequently improve student learning. Prior experience has shown that students will generally give each other strong, positive ratings and sometimes give all team members the identical rating, unless the importance of feedback is stressed and they are coached on how to evaluate each other. Repeated use of a peer evaluation rubric at key points in the project will encourage students to give realistic appraisals of each others' contributions to the project. By the end of the semester, the instructor may have increased confidence in the validity of the reports and include peer reviews in determining individual's course grade. See Appendix for BESTEAMS Peer Evaluation Form.

Instructors can give more credibility to the peer ratings by insisting that students who receive low peer ratings, especially in the early days of the team's life, seek specific feedback and develop a plan for improvement. Since most peer ratings are anonymous and the teacher's feedback is based (totally or in part) upon the peer ratings, the student with the low rating should be prompted to go back to the team to discuss the reasons for the low ratings. Alternatively, the student may turn to the instructor for an explanation, which again can open a productive dialogue about expected team behaviors and the importance of peer feedback.

Can you assess too much? As dangerously unreliable as the single/peer team rating can be, requesting team or peer feedback too frequently is also ineffective and burdensome for the team. Students may stop taking the assessments seriously if they occur too often, especially if there is not enough time for the team to act or to work through team issues.

The actual percentage the instructor uses to weigh the team contribution to the grade compared to the individual efforts should be carefully considered. Less experienced students may not feel as threatened if a significant part of their grade is still within their own control. On the other hand, capstone courses often assume that students have had many prior team experiences and attempt to prepare students for the real world they are about to enter by grading solely on the completed project. In the former case, students on the same team could have different grades, whereas they probably would not in the senior capstone course.

A related concern is the instructor's desire that each student master all the important subject content connected to the team project. As noted above, engineering students run the risk of becoming project specialists at the expense of broader learning unless the instructor intervenes. Strategies for ensuring subject mastery include separate examinations related to project content and oral examinations where students are individually asked questions related to the project but outside their specific role. Alternatively, instructors can require that students trade team roles during the project so that students participate in a variety of activities and increase the breadth of their experience.

With regard to project success and grading, most instructors take the position that the key outcome is learning and important learning can occur in the context of project failure. Indeed, sometimes the most effective way to learn is by making mistakes. Again, the professor should be clear in the initial class and syllabus how much of a student's grade will be determined by a successful team project versus a valiant attempt.

In the moment: Dealing with the problem in real time

What if, despite the faculty member's best efforts at clearly outlining expectations for grading early in the semester, students come forward with problems about their team grade? What can be done?

Determine the source of the dissatisfaction: Is the basis for the student's unhappiness disappointment with the team or with his or her own performance?

- If dissatisfied with the team or team grade, look to the peer evaluations for insight. What do they suggest about the team process and accomplishments? Was this individual dragged down by the others, despite his or her best efforts? Even so, is that a reason for adjusting the student's grade? Were team expectations clear? Check the team charter or a similar document to verify the student met specified expectations.

- If the individual is disappointed in his or her own performance, consider what is going on in the student's life. Are there compelling mitigating circumstances that influenced how well this student could perform? Are there ways for the student to make up work or complete extra credit that would increase learning and be meaningful?

Clarify team goals and expectations: If multiple students are unhappy with their grades, consider holding a team meeting. Again, examine the source(s) of the discomfort and proceed by checking expectations and behaviors, and asking students for their input into the solution. While students may never be completely satisfied with their final project grade, turning this into a teachable moment will encourage them to address problems more immediately in the future, as well as clearly outline their expectations for team performance. Learning how to work well on a team is not easy; reminding students that this is a lifelong skill they are developing will hopefully place their experience within a larger context.

2.4 Managing "slackers" or non-contributing team members

One of the most common problems for students on engineering teams is the non-participating member. Slacker behavior includes not showing up for meetings, being unprepared, and wasting time with non-project related talk or activity. Slackers demoralize the team, hamper team progress, and are the source of subtle and not-so-subtle group conflicts. Below are some suggestions for addressing this issue.

Heading off the issue: Preemptive steps

Preventive strategies that ensure full team participation include the following:

Identify clear team roles: These positions should be rotated on a planned schedule with specific responsibilities. There are many roles that may be played in a group, but the following three roles are necessary at a minimum: Leader, Member, and Facilitator.

The leader directs the group, builds consensus, and keeps the final goal in sight. The members contribute their own individual expertise to the achievement of the final project. The facilitator pays attention to the group process and dynamics, encourages the use of constructive feedback and good listening skills, and assists in conflict management.

Requiring each member of a team to play each role on a rotating basis assists in full team participation. Establishing consensus as the goal for group decision-making also sets the stage for involvement by all team members.

Ensure student grades include team contributions: Grades earned must represent the contribution to team activities. Instructors should be clear about how individual work and team work will be evaluated when determining the student's final grade. If zero percent of the grade depends on team participation, then slackers have no consequence for their behaviors. Likewise, students must be taught about the importance of team feedback and team evaluations. Instructors should ask teams to evaluate each other at least several times during the semester, especially after the first team deliverable (see Appendix for the Team Evaluation Form). In addition, having the expectation that work must be turned in within the deadline acts as a deterrent to the slackers and disorganized members of the class. The negative consequences to the team, and the resulting peer pressure, usually result in on-time participation.

Build "get acquainted" activities into the class early in the semester: Successful team experiences require a high degree of trust. Especially with newly formed teams where individuals have had little experience with one another, developing team identity and comfort is important. For example, some teams begin by creating a team name and logo. Participation in team training activities such as creativity training or group dynamics early in the semester gives team members a chance to get to know each other. These activities especially help quiet and shy students become acquainted with their team members in a less stressful environment than working on the graded team project.

Have students discuss and prepare guidelines for the operation of their team: Some teams accomplish this by writing a formal group charter while others create a simple list of acceptable team behaviors and expectations. Among the team expectations, establish the ground rule that it is important to hear from everyone in the group. To encourage this, break into subgroups to discuss some issues, than have the subgroups come together to share their ideas. Alternatively, ask everyone to take a few minutes of silent thinking time before making a decision or taking action. The silent time will help the students to organize their thoughts before speaking.

In the moment: Dealing with the problem in real time

If all the advanced planning did not work, what can be done now?

Have teammates approach the slacker: Encourage the team members to directly ask what is causing the person to be inactive. Are there issues that can be resolved with team or instructor assistance? For some students, withdrawal may be seen as the best solution to a situation. For example, is the student incompatible with another team member and afraid to talk about it? Is there a problem at home that causes the team member to miss meetings?

Instructor intervention: Use the peer evaluation material as the basis of discussion with the non-participating student. This serves two purposes. First, it demonstrates the value of the peer evaluation to both the students and to the instructor in providing concrete feedback that is useful in managing group dynamics. Second, using the peer evaluation provides specifics that can be used to address the individual slacker's problem (the peer evaluation form can ask for suggestions to remedy the behavior problems). Use feedback sessions early on to identify, understand, and help change problem behaviors. In addition, some instructors require their students to keep team minutes where they document each member's responsibilities and the actions taken. Students who are absent from group meetings are noted. Instructors may impose penalties that were fully disclosed in the course syllabus, such as losing points or lowering grades as a result of poor team participation.

Fire a team member: If the slacker behavior continues, despite various interventions such as those previously suggested, the team may have the option of firing the offending team member. Usually documentation of performance failure is required such as team minutes, peer evaluations, and attendance records. "Firing" a team member can be approached in several ways, including giving teams the option from the beginning of the project or requiring team members to petition the instructor to take such an action. Students who are fired can be assigned to other teams, asked to do equivalent work one-on-one with the instructor as supervisor, or even asked to retake the course at another time.

Form a team of slackers: Especially in upper level courses, where students are familiar with each other and perhaps have worked together on teams before, students who have a poor reputation for teamwork are often well known to their peers. This information may come to the attention of the instructor during the team formation stage of the project when various students plead "not to be assigned to a team with him/her!" A novel strategy is to assign all "problem" students to one team. Without the usual rescuers around, these students will have to become involved in the team project to be successful in the course. Instructors can provide special coaching or assistance from teaching assistants to that group.

In some academic cultures, students will protect slackers and their negative behavior may not come to the attention of the teacher until after the project has been completed. In that case, there is little the instructor can do except be aware of the culture and in the heading off phase with the next team project class, point out that carrying slackers serves neither the team nor the slacker. Everyone's learning and experience is impaired.

2.5 Dealing with dysfunctional teams

Sometimes, despite the best efforts of the instructor, teams do not function well. Consistent with the well-known Pareto TQM principle, that 20% of the sources cause 80% of the problems, even one dysfunctional student project team can take 80% of the instructor's time to resolve. Therefore, having tools or guidelines for helping dysfunctional teams work through their process is necessary. This book emphasizes people versus project breakdown issues. Engineering faculty members are usually well versed in handling technical project difficulties, such as design, manufacture, and sustainability.

Heading off the issue: Pre-emptive steps

Before declaring disaster, consider the following:

Provide increased or additional team training for the entire class: If the instructor is aware of one dysfunctional team, there may be others that also are floundering. Therefore, "just in time" training might assist everyone. Pertinent topics include:

- Giving and receiving feedback
- Team chartering to establish ground rules for the team
- Creating a project timeline that establishes ongoing milestones for project completion
- Conflict management training

Meet with individual team members to discuss the situation: Perhaps getting more involved in the team can prevent small problems from turning into big ones. This is particularly useful with inexperienced teams or those in their early stages of development. Have you considered acting as a team consultant rather than instructor or evaluator? Meet with team members individually first and then as a group to guide them toward smoother functioning.

Determine where the team is in terms of typical stages of development (e.g., forming, storming, norming, performing, or adjourning): If the team is appropriately storming, your best bet is to help the team appreciate the importance of this stage, which leads to performing, and offer some tips on how they can manage the process. For more information on this issue, see "Theoretical Foundations" of the Introductory Interpersonal module.

In the moment: Dealing with the problem in real time

If a team requires more intrusive intervention to get it back on track, here are some suggestions for identifying and solving common team problems. Adapted from Scholtes (1988).

Aimlessness: Indicated by indecision, false starts, directionless discussions, postponed decisions, and lack of follow-through. This may occur because team is overwhelmed, there is a lack of consensus on how to proceed, or team is reluctant to finish and disband.

Ask the team to review how their project is being run ("let's review the charge/mission/task and see if everyone is clear") and ask probing questions ("what needs to happen so the group can move on?" or "what do you think is holding the team up?"). Also ask "what's missing?" Consensus? Data? Information? Support? Unacknowledged feelings?

Dictatorial participants: Indicated by "experts" exerting too much influence in the group; "untouchability" of his or her ideas; and discounting others' experiences and suggestions.
Establish that everyone is a part of the process and no area is off limits. Ask the expert to share expertise and not ultimatums so the rest of the group can be empowered, and reinforce importance of data (and not just expert opinion) in making progress on the project.

Overbearing participants: Indicated by group members who spend more time than is welcome speaking (or lecturing) during team meetings, dominate the team interactions, and do not listen to others.

Structure the discussion so that everyone gets to speak: use round robins, ask members to write down thoughts and share, and evaluate group process (ask the question: "does everyone participate?").

Unwilling participants: Indicated by group members who do not speak (opposite of overbearing), who are shy or unsure of themselves, and who rarely volunteer or act.

Same as overbearing participants. Assign specific assignments or duties and ask the individual directly for input.

Confusing opinions with facts: Indicated by team members who express their opinions with such assurance that other members are reluctant to question their points of view for fear of appearing impolite or wrong.

Suggest group members ask directly, "is what you said an opinion or fact?" or "Do you have data?" (Scholtes, p. 6-41). Review the importance of all group members understanding and engaging in consensus based actions grounded in mutually understood evidence.

Rushing to conclusion: Indicated by at least one action-oriented member who pressures the group into premature action. This individual is impatient with the scientific process and may discount group process activities in exchange for the need to solve the problem.

Remind the team of the planned process and the need to proceed systematically; talk to the individual, pointing out examples of rushing and the impact this has on the work of the group.

(Mis)Attribution: Indicated by labeling another's behavior due to a misunderstanding or attributing motives to others without data or information ("he's just lazy/waiting for others to do the work").

Establish the need for evidence at all junctures: ask "how do you know that?" or "Can this be validated with hard evidence?" Ask the individuals being (mis)attributed how they would describe his or her intentions ("How would you describe what was just said?" or "Is this what you meant?").

Disregarded ideas: Indicated by the discounting of other members statements and opinions; the team ignores input and moves on without acknowledging the member's contribution.

Reinforce that all members' contributions need to be acknowledged, even the ones that seem useless or do not make sense. Seek clarification; use active listening (e.g., follow-up questions); ask the individual, "before the team moves on, should we spend more time on this idea? Can you help us see where this fits or helps the discussion?" Remind all group members that the use of constructive feedback and active listening are key to good group functioning.

Tangents: Indicated by wide-ranging, unfocused but enthusiastic discussions that stray from the project.

Suggest that the team create an agenda at the beginning of each meeting by agreeing on a list of points and topics to be covered and referred back to as necessary. Identify one "traffic cop" whose job is to direct members back to the topic ("We've moved away from the topic, let's get back on track"). Ask the team to discover if they are avoiding the work and ask why: "Since the team has difficulty maintaining focus on this topic, is there something about it that enables avoidance?" (e.g., inability to do the work or fear of change).

Feuding team members: Indicated by overt conflict between a subset of team members that disrupts the entire team.

Discuss the problem outside of the team meeting. Encourage combatants to agree to manage their differences outside the team without disrupting the group. Offering to facilitate the dialogue may speed the conflict resolution. Review conflict management skills and stress the equal importance of completing the team project/product and having successful group processes.

If the instructor agrees that learning team dynamics skills is an important part of participating in an engineering project team, then the question of who should deal with the team problems becomes important. Is the instructor the appropriate choice, or should the team members work things out for themselves?

Our suggestion is to take into account the level of team sophistication of the students involved. Young students or those relatively inexperienced with teamwork might most benefit from instructor intervention and specific training in team skills. Older, more experienced teams might be asked to handle things more autonomously. In such cases, the instructor might coach the team leader on various strategies for handling the problem(s) that have arisen.

2.6 Maximizing the team experience for women and other underrepresented groups

Engineering as a field has a history of being predominantly white and male in the United States. Our society is constantly changing, with increasing percentages of women, people of color, and immigrants. As a result, jobs too have changed with a dramatic increased need for talented engineers and technically savvy individuals. Therefore, engineering educators will face more and more diverse classrooms as well as pressure to effectively teach as many future technology professionals as possible. It is important to note that diversity includes any characteristic that differentiates people from the mainstream population. Culture, disability, religion, language, age, sexual orientation, and socio-economic background are other ways in which students can be in the minority. In the present context the focus will be on issues related to student project teams and women and students of color. Below are some suggestions for making the engineering classroom an effective learning environment for all students.

Heading off the issue: Preemptive steps

Build diversity awareness into team training: Especially in the beginning of the course, never miss an opportunity to stress the increasing internationalization of engineering as a field, the importance of working with diverse others as a requirement of professional work, and the notion that the diverse team usually makes a better product or outcome. The notion of *Groupthink*, defined as pressured consensus that masks real differences of opinion, can result in catastrophic failures (Janis, 1982). The Challenger space shuttle's commission investigation, which revealed knowledge of serious potential problems that were not sufficient to prevent the launch, may be a useful illustration in this discussion. See Rounds (2000) for further information on this particular issue.

Include diversity appreciation as a component in team chartering: In writing team charters, urge students to consider:

- Issues of communication with the goal of promoting effective interactions among all members
- Specific ground rules that apply to all team members, for example, expectations for participation and acceptance of team rules
- Valuing each team member's unique strengths and weaknesses. Make the commitment that stereotypes of any kind are not allowed to interfere with team operation.

Include team building exercises: Encouraging students to get past their first assumptions, creating common ground, and establishing trust is vital to the functioning of diverse teams. Especially in first year and sophomore classes where students are less familiar with each other, consider ice-breakers and team building exercises so students can get to know each other as individuals. Exercises that are related to engineering are particularly appropriate (e.g., providing students with a set of materials such as paperclips, string, rubber bands and note paper and asking them to collaborate on an outcome such as projecting the paperclip the greatest distance, putting together the longest chain, or sustaining the greatest weight). For additional ideas, see Jones (2002).

Use strategic team member assignment: This method, discussed previously in section 2.2, encourages the inclusion of underrepresented groups. It also works to ensure that the team experience is positive for potentially marginalized students.

In the moment: Dealing with the problem in real time

As a first step, remember that team conflict can be useful and is indeed predictable at a certain stage of the team's development (e.g., "storming"). Diversity conflict has special features but can also benefit from the techniques, skills, and training needed to manage general conflict in teams.

Identify the source of conflict: Interpersonal conflicts related to diversity often come down to three issues: a) value differences, b) expectation differences, and c) perception differences. Adapted from Myers (1996).

- **Value differences:** While there may be many different values, those that impact team effectiveness often relate to differences regarding work ethic, understanding of authority, outlook on age/maturity, individual versus team goals and personal recognition, and role and expression of feelings in the work/team environment.

- **Expectation differences:** These differences refer to what people expect from themselves and others based on their own personal and culturally based characteristics, as well as their values and perceptions. Examples include stereotypes (expecting team members to be more or less skilled based on stereotypes rather than direct knowledge of the individuals); sanctity of work roles and chain of command; degree of personal sharing; personal involvement and interest expected from teammates; and expectation that others will value and reward good work without vigorous self-promotion.

- **Perception differences:** These differences refer to how people perceive situations based on their own early environments and childhood experiences. Examples include regional differences and accents or dialects (e.g., using street language means a person is not intelligent); personal space requirements (e.g., some cultures value closeness and proximity when speaking... others find standing too close during conversation intimidating); and individual notions of propriety (e.g., some team members may feel more comfortable discussing problems with a teaching assistant rather than an instructor because of perceptions of formality and authority).

Resolve the issue after identifying the nature of the problem: Focus on communication, checking assumptions about team members, and conflict resolution skills. As communication and conflict management skills are discussed in segment 4.2 of this book, the current section focuses on checking assumptions.

- In order to help identify assumptions, ask students to consider what their parents or grandparents would say about a particular person or situation. Can they recognize unfounded attributes or characteristics that come up from their personal histories?

- Remind students to be careful of generalizing from one person or experience to a whole group.

- Suggest that when challenging assumptions, new data should be sought. Some probing questions include: How has the person performed on other teams? Do others on the team feel similarly or differently? What do the observers base their opinion on?

- As a result of new data or insights, are students willing to change their minds? Switching to a new perception or idea may be crucial to the future performance of the team.

In sum, learning to be an effective team player is not automatic for professors *or* students. Much thought should go into the choices made and even then there is no guarantee that everything will run smoothly. The topics addressed above provide the foundation for faculty members who wish to help their students develop well-functioning engineering teams. For more information on this subject, see the sources cited.

2.7 Sources Cited

Janis, I. (1982). *Groupthink* (2nd ed). Boston: Houghton Mifflin.

Jones, A. (2002). *More team-building activities for every group.* Rec. Room Publishing.

Myers, S.G. (1996). *Team building for diverse work groups: A practical guide to gaining and sustaining performance in diverse teams.* Irvine, CA: Richard Chang Associates, Inc.

Rounds, J. (2000). *Groupthink.* Retrieved November 19, 2004, from http://www.colostate.edu/Depts/Speech/rccs/theory16.htm

Scholtes, P.R. (1988). *The team handbook: How to use teams to improve quality.* Madison, WI: Joiner Associates Inc.

Chapter 3 BESTEAMS MODULE PERSONAL KNOWLEDGE

3.1 Introduction to Module

This Module Implementation Plan (MIP) has been crafted to enhance students' understanding regarding their own preferences as learners and members of engineering teams. New engineering students often lack the self-knowledge required to effectively work on project teams. They may not appreciate how knowing their own strengths will allow them to find the right fit within a team as well as to use the strengths of others to maximize team learning and performance. One tool to assist students in increasing their personal knowledge is the Kolb Learning Style Inventory (LSI). The LSI measures learning styles.

Learning styles are preferred ways of learning and engaging in educational practices (see the section below). BESTEAMS selected Kolb's Learning Style Inventory (Kolb, 1999) as the basis of this module for the following reasons:

- Administration of the Kolb LSI is straightforward and allows for easy assessment
- Understanding style differences influences member-to-member and team-to-member interactions
- Understanding style differences influences faculty-to-student and faculty-to-class interactions
- Learning styles reflect a relevant aspect of diversity present in many engineering teams and allows students to consider individual differences beyond those of race and gender

3.2 David Kolb's Experiential Learning Model: Theoretical Foundations

David Kolb's Experiential Learning Model resides within a long tradition of theory that seeks to explain how participatory learning and the environment affect student learning outcomes. Prominent theorists who have explored these ideas include Dewey (1958), Lewin (1951), and Piaget (1971). Kolb's work considers those who preceded him, and offers an explanation for, in his own words, "how experience is translated into concepts, which, in turn, are used as guides in the choice of new experiences" (Kolb, 1981, p. 235). According to his work, the ways individuals learn and the subjects they study are directly related to their learning preferences.

At the center of the model are two basic dimensions of learning: the active-reflective and the abstract-concrete preferences. The active-reflective preference refers to the degree to which a student prefers to process new information, either by "actively" engaging the material or by "reflectively" considering it. For example, it is common place to hear engineering students say that they learn best by taking things apart and putting things back together. This could be described as an active learning preference. In contrast, the student who prefers to read about a phenomena, watch a demonstration, and then reflect on his/her internal understandings of the new material could be said to have a reflective learning preference. The LSI places the learner along a continuum of preference. Students can be strong or weak in their preferences for active/reflective processing of new information.

Kolb's other key dimension of learning differences has to do with how students prefer to use or act on the new material they have processed. The concrete to abstract continuum suggests that students differ in their preferences for applying new knowledge and insights to the "real world" versus more theoretical pursuits such as theory building. Again, many engineering students prefer "concrete" learning applications, which should come as no surprise since engineering is largely an applied field. Physicists, on the other hand, are more likely to prefer abstract learning uses, such as applying new knowledge to the extension of non-measurable events (e.g., how black holes are created) or theory development. Kolb named the extremes on the two continuums as follows: active experimentation (AE) to reflective observation (RO), and concrete experience (CE) to abstract conceptualization (AC) (Kolb, 1999).

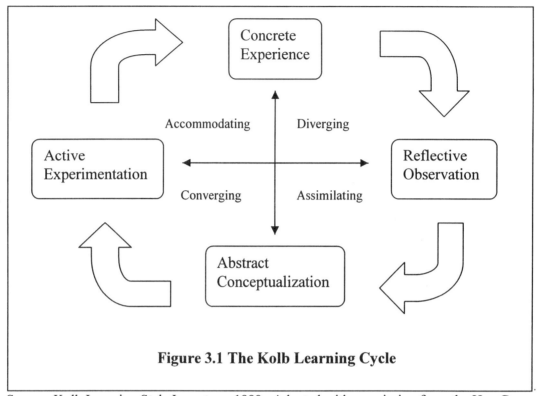

Figure 3.1 The Kolb Learning Cycle

Source: Kolb Learning Style Inventory, 1999. Adapted with permission from the Hay Group.

Each individual has a preference for processing information and then using or judging the perceived data. Kolb formed four learning styles based upon combinations of the abstract-concrete and active-reflective dimensions. The individual with a diverging learning style preference (high CE and RO preferences) excels when brainstorming ideas, viewing issues from a variety of perspectives, developing alternative solutions, and relating to other people. This individual's strong person-oriented drive enables him or her to note others' feelings and to value diverse perspectives. The Diverger's weakness is that indecision may set in as he or she attempts to incorporate all views and everyone's feelings; the individual may become overwhelmed with too many possibilities (Evans, Forney, & Guido-DiBrito, 1998).

Assimilating learning style preference (high RO and AC) learners excel at inductive reasoning and prefer to examine a problem and develop theories based on the issue at hand. They gain their name from their ability to assimilate numerous pieces of data into a coherent whole (Claxton & Murrell, 1987). The Assimilator values ideas for their logical soundness, which may lead him or her to sacrifice practicality in return for theoretical perfection. Consequently, Assimilators may have difficulty taking action once a problem is identified.

The third learning style, converging, comes from the interplay of high AC and AE. The Converger's strength is in the application of an idea to a particular situation, especially when there is one right answer. This skill serves the Converger well on standardized tests and in situations where a decision must be made. This same skill, however, can lead the Converger to make premature decisions and even solve the wrong problem (Evans et al., 1998). This learning style is particularly important when teaching engineering classes, for these students are disproportionately Convergers. While the Convergers' positive qualities are often what make them excel technically, they may lack appreciation of or motivation to develop professional skills. Subsequently, it is vital that instructors ensure Convergers are learning how to work well with others who may not share their learning style, as well as mastering the technical skills necessary to complete engineering projects.

The accommodating learning style is a combination of high AE and CE. These individuals are most comfortable learning by trial and error and they excel in implementing tasks and completing projects. Unfortunately, this "rush to get done" attitude may come at a cost—the Accommodator may become caught up in activity for activity's sake, leading him or her to perform unnecessary or insignificant tasks (Evans et al., 1998).

Not only did Kolb (1981) capture these learning style preferences, he found that as students learn, they move "in varying degrees from actor to observer, from specific involvement to general analytic detachment" or what he termed the "learning cycle" (p. 236) (see fig. 3.1). Although one may enter the cycle at any point, learning usually begins with a specific experience (CE), then moves through a watching/reflective phase (RO), into a thinking period (AC) and concludes on an active note (AE). Each stage provides the foundation for the next and as individuals learn, they will cycle through these stages repeatedly, creating what some practitioners call the "learning spiral" (Stewart, 1990). In learning, all four approaches to processing and applying information are important to the mastery of new material.

Kolb (1981) has further observed that complete mastery of these four elements by any one person is complicated by the different skills required for the various types of learning. This is particularly true for the learning quadrant that is directly opposite an individual's most preferred learning style. For example, an Accommodator who is comfortable developing a solution to a problem immediately may find herself extremely ill at ease when thinking about the theory behind the action that she would like to take. Conversely, an Assimilator would eagerly perform the latter task, while potentially neglecting the former. The same holds true for Convergers and Divergers: students who excel in one type of learning may need to be encouraged to explore the other quadrants.

One method of supporting students in becoming fluent in all four learning areas is to encourage exploration of their own preferred learning style. To this end, Kolb developed the Learning Styles Inventory (LSI), a short questionnaire to determine learning style preferences. There have been multiple iterations of the LSI over the past twenty years; the most recent version was released in 1999. The LSI consists of twelve stem completions that students rank according to their learning preferences. The answers to these questions then provide scores for each of the four processes: concrete experience (CE), reflective observation (RO), abstract conceptualization (AC), and active experimentation (AE). When AC is subtracted from CE and AE is subtracted from RO, the result is a set of coordinates that identifies the individual's learning style preference (Kolb, 1981).

Much research has been performed regarding the utility of the LSI. In general, Kolb and his critics have agreed that the LSI is most useful for promoting self-awareness about learning preferences rather than acting as a diagnostic tool (Atkinson, 1991; Claxton & Murrell, 1987). Indeed, instructors who introduce Kolb's Learning Styles Model may be well served to remind students that LSI results should not be used as a tool to pigeon-hole their classmates. There is also the potential that results may not match those which a student expects. Sometimes this maybe a sign that a student incorrectly followed the instructions for completing the instrument (the most common error is reversing the 1-4 ranking scale). If this is not the case, students should be asked what they think their preferred learning style is, and not forced to accept the findings of the instrument. In any case, information gleaned from the completion of the LSI may still be used to promote awareness and reflection in the classroom and team environments.

How does using the LSI improve engineering teamwork? Kolb (1999) maintains that all four learning styles are important for the complete learning cycle to take place. However, students naturally rely on the learning style for which they have the most affinity. As noted above, in the case of engineers, the majority of them tend to be Convergers—this may not be surprising, for engineering is a field that revolves around the completion of technical tasks and problem solving. However, the Converger also tends to be project-oriented rather than person-oriented, a trait that may result in a satisfactory final product, but can also lead to very trying times in the interpersonally oriented group setting. Subsequently, knowing Kolb types on teams can in turn suggest *team* strengths and weaknesses.

There are two issues at stake when considering the LSI and engineering teams. First, taking the LSI and discussing its results can encourage students to consider the quadrants of the learning cycle where they are weakest. Oftentimes, just bringing attention to the ways in which learning occurs can motivate students to consider how they might learn better and more effectively. Second, use of the LSI will begin to teach students to recognize differences as strengths, which is particularly important in a mixed-learning styles group. Understanding this information may help members of a team recognize the relative strengths of each of four quadrants and attempt to apply these perspectives in team activities, from brainstorming to project report completion. Awareness of different Kolb strengths is particularly useful if the group is heavily slanted toward one learning style, as is often the case with engineering classes. Students can ask, what would the missing style say about the topic under consideration? In other words, "what would a Diverger contribute to this decision?" or "what would an accommodating view point contribute to solving this problem?"

Utilizing the LSI will serve to improve learning as the individuals appreciate their own strengths and weakness, act as a positive diversity filter for students to interpret differences in team members, and assist instructors in becoming more effective teachers by considering the value of "learning around the cycle" to meet the learning style preferences of all of their students.

Finally, the increased personal awareness facilitated by this module teaches students how to be more effective lifelong learners. While the need for this skill may not be immediately apparent to students, faculty will recognize its importance, for changes in the workplace and scholarship have underscored the importance of this ability.

3.3 Sources Cited

Claxton, C.S. & Murrell, P.H. (1987). Learning styles: Implications for improving educational practices. *ASHE-ERIC Higher Education Report*, No. 4.

Dewey, J. (1958). *Experience and nature* (2nd ed.). La Salle, IL: Open Court.

Evans, N.J., Forney, D.S., & Guido-DiBrito, F. (1998). *Student development in college.* San Francisco: Jossey-Bass.

Kolb, D.A. (1981). Learning styles and disciplinary differences. In A. Chickering (Ed.), *The American modern college* (pp. 232-255). San Francisco: Jossey-Bass.

Kolb, D.A. (1999). *The Kolb Learning Style Inventory (ver. 3).* Boston: Hay Group.

Lewin, K. (1951). *Field theory in the social sciences*. New York: Harper & Row.

Myers, I.B. (1976). *Introduction to type*. Gainsville, FL: Center for the Application of Psychological Type.

Piaget, J. (1971). *Psychology and epistemology* (A. Rosin, Trans.). New York: Grossman.

Stewart, G.M. (1990, Summer). Learning styles as a filter for developing service-learning Interventions. *New Directions for Student Services*, 50.

3.4 50-Minute Class Overview: Understanding Your Learning Style I Personal Knowledge

Module Outline
- Introduce objectives of lesson
- Ask broad questions to generate discussion
- Administer the LSI (as needed)
- Deliver formal lecture on Kolb
- Divide class by learning types and have groups complete pre-determined task
- Facilitate class discussion: how will knowing this information change the way individuals relate in the future?

Expected student outcomes
- Insight into learning style preferences and their strengths
- Insight into differences beyond those typically measured
- Insight into how learning and communication style preferences influence the reception, delivery, and processing of technical material

Assessment/Homework Options
- Add questions in midterm or final exam
- Follow-up questionnaire
- Assign Learning Style/team work reading assignment: instructor choice
- Assign reflective writing assignment

Materials Needed
- PowerPoint Slides
- Computer
- Projector
- LSI
- Large sheets of paper for groups
- Markers to use for writing on paper

90-Minute Class Overview: Extended Class Outline & Additional Outcomes

Extended Class Outline
- In teams: Students explore expected behaviors in teams
- In teams: Students identify their teammates' learning styles
- In teams: Students identify team strengths and challenges

Additional Expected Outcomes
- Insight into how Learning Styles affect team dynamics
- Insight into ways to minimize team weaknesses and capitalize on team strengths
- Insight into the rotation around the learning cycle

3.5 BESTEAMS Module Implementation Plan (MIP)
Introductory Level Personal Knowledge

Topic: *Diversity in Learning Styles*

Tracks	Personal Knowledge	Interpersonal Effectiveness	Project Management
Introductory	Kolb Learning Styles	Team Development & Communications Basics	Managing Your Project: Planning & Time

Introduction/Motivation

As engineering educators work to ensure their students are learning the skills industry now requires of its professionals, innovative strategies are developing to meet this need. This module teaches students to recognize their personal learning preferences so they may use that knowledge to participate in an effective team environment. Understanding the individual's strengths is vital before team members are able to synthesize their talents into something greater than a solitary project. Utilizing Kolb's Learning Styles Inventory (LSI) will enable individuals to understand their own preferences, and is a first step toward appreciating one aspect of the diversity inherent in teams.

This Module Implementation Plan (MIP) is structured to ensure that the material will resonate with students of all learning style preferences—Divergering, Assimilating, Converging, and Accommodating alike. By "teaching around the cycle" in the delivery of this material, instructors provide information accessible to all learners as well as increase student awareness of other learning style preferences.

The complete PowerPoint® presentation shown in this module is available for download at **http://www.enme.umd.edu/labs/BESTEAMS/**

Expected Outcomes

Upon implementation of this module, students should achieve numerous outcomes that facilitate the development of useful team skills, including:

Module Part I

- Insight into their own learning style .preferences, as defined by the Kolb Learning Style Inventory, as well as an appreciation for strengths of all learning styles

- Insight into the differences beyond those typically measured that are present in an engineering classroom
- Insight into how learning and communication style preferences influence the reception, delivery, and processing of technical information

Module Part II

- Insight into how learning styles affect team dynamics
- Insight into using learning styles in teamwork, particularly to minimize team weaknesses and maximize team strengths
- Insight into understanding that good problem solving and effective teamwork result from a complete circuit of the learning cycle

Delivery Plan for Part I: Designed for a 50-minute class period

Introduce the module and the objectives of the session. Class characteristics should be considered when determining how best to present the expected outcomes from above. For example, a group of first-year students may be most interested in identifying their own learning styles. The instructor can emphasize the need for students to be aware of their own learning style so that they can take a preferred approach when facing new material. Students who know their preferred learning style can also ask the instructor questions designed to match that strength.

Personal Knowledge Learning Objectives

- Understanding of personal learning style preference
- Awareness of non-traditional measures of difference, beyond superficial generalizations
- Knowledge of how these differences affect the reception and processing of information

---

Introduction to Learning Styles

Begin exploring learning styles through discussion of the module's utility. This section is designed to encourage thought about learning styles. The activities will naturally appeal to the Divergers in the class, who are driven to learn by asking the question, "why?"

The Kolb LSI is one type of attribute filter that helps individuals make sense of groupings of people. The benefits of using learning styles in team training are numerous. For students, identification of an individual's style helps the student understand him or herself as a learner.

Appreciating Learning Styles

- Knowing strengths is important for effective team members
- Attribute filters are sets of characteristics used to define similarity groups
  - Examples: Gender, Myers-Briggs Personality Types, SAT scores, GPA
- We use attribute filters to learn about ourselves and how to relate to diverse others

---

Likewise, understanding style differences improves member-to-member and team-to-member interactions. For faculty members, one of the benefits is that a short, reliable, easy-to-interpret measure exists for determining learning styles. Additionally, understanding style differences improves faculty-student and faculty-class interactions.

Encourage students to consider why discussing learning styles might be useful in an engineering context.

Engage in higher level or what is sometimes called "Socratic" questioning. For example the instructor may ask open ended questions such as the following:

> Why is it hard to explain something about engineering to someone in a non-technical field?

> How can some of your friends tell you are an engineering student just by the way you explain a topic?

The intention is to draw the students into a conversation about the issues and develop their awareness of individual differences.

Activity: Sharing personal experience

Relate a personal experience where you were having difficulty communicating an idea to a student in class and explain how the impasse was resolved. For example, it is sometimes useful to have students draw a diagram to help the instructor understand their question. Alternatively, using a specific example can illustrate their area of confusion and clear up the misunderstanding.

We all perceive, learn, and experience reality differently. Team members are challenged to use these differences to their advantage in the completion of the team project and as they work to make the most of student-instructor interactions.

Kolb's LSI

Administer the Kolb LSI and provide theoretical background information for students on Kolb's LSI. Information delivered in this section will demonstrate the larger theoretical framework within which Kolb's work rests, as well as lead students to see the way this material may be utilized in their own lives, and teamwork experiences. The activities will appeal to Assimilators in the class, who are driven to learn by asking the question, "what?" Completing the LSI will also appeal to Convergers, who want to get to the "doing."

If class time is short, it is also acceptable to assign the LSI as homework. This allows the instructor to move directly into the Kolb lecture.

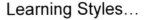

Learning Styles...

- Describe the way you *prefer* to learn
- Influence how you deal with day-to-day interactions and tasks
- Are determined by reflecting on your preference for doing specific tasks

Think of the last time you dealt with new technical information…
How do you best like to learn?

Completing the Kolb Learning Style Inventory (LSI)

Answer the 12 questions in the LSI
- Forced ranking (no ties)
  4= Most like you
  1= Least like you
- Follow the instructions on "The Cycle of Learning" page in the Kolb booklet
  - Determine your CE, RO, AC, & AE scores
  - Plot them on the cycle and fill in the resul kite shape

Understanding Your Preferences

- What does your learning style kite tell you?
  - You are unique (compare kites)
  - The length of kite "arms" indicate the strength of your preference for that interaction

Completing the LSI

Have students follow the instructions on "The Cycle of Learning" page in the instrument. Students should determine CE, RO, AC, and AE scores and plot their scores, resulting in a 4-sided "kite" shape.

Have students shade in their kite shapes and hold up their diagrams to demonstrate the visible differences in learning styles as captured by the Kolb LSI. What differences do they see? For example, equally balanced kites suggest no strongly preferred learning style. Narrow kites or those with a long "arm" suggest that a student is "less comfortable" in the narrow dimension and strongly prefers the long arm means of learning and interacting.

 Instructors must be aware of the students who are in a minority learning style. A sole Diverger or Accommodator in an introductory engineering class may be uncomfortable. The instructor can mitigate this by foreshadowing the importance of learning around the cycle and by mentioning that the most successful teams often consist of those with heterogeneous learning styles.

Kolb Lecture

Resources for this lecture include PowerPoint® presentation slides (available at **http://www.enme.umd.edu/labs/BESTEAMS/**) and background reading materials whose citations are provided in this section. Much has been published on Kolb. For more information, see section 3.2 of this book; the learning style references list at the end of the MIP; or search "David A. Kolb" on the Internet.

Learning Styles

- The Kolb Learning Style highlights your preference for:
  - Concrete experience (sensing)
  - Abstract conceptualization (thinking)
  - Reflective observation (watching)
  - Active experimentation (doing)
- These are methods of perceiving and processing information
- Kolb defined four learning styles as combinations of these modes

Information Perceiving Styles

- **Concrete experience (CE)** – Learner is immersed in the new experience by being open, adaptive, and maximizing involvement. Sensing and valuing the experience dominate learner's interaction.
- **Abstract conceptualization (AC)** – Learner logically and systematically organizes the information into concepts and ideas. Building a general theory out of the experience is important to the learner.

During this lecture, the instructor assists the students in completing the LSI (as needed) and presents a description of each learning style along with its strengths and challenges. This slide and the next succinctly describe the four Kolb dimensions. Sharing the Kolb figure (figure 3.1) from the Theoretical Foundations section may prove useful in providing a graphic representation of these concepts.

Recall the perceiving dimension refers to how the individual takes in information from the physical world. Once having absorbed the data, students must "make decisions" about how to use this information, or the processing function.

Information Processing Styles

- **Reflective observation (RO)** – Learner is the objective observer, viewing the experience from many different perspectives. The learner is patiently watching and thinking.
- **Active experimentation (AE)** – Learner is directly involved in the occurrence, interacting with the environment in and around the experience.

Taken together, these four information learning dimensions should reflect the styles of all members of the class. Students will differ in their strength of preference for each dimension. For example, some engineers will exhibit a high preference for active experimentation as their primary information style.

Later in the presentation the instructor should emphasize the importance of all learning dimensions in teamwork and problem solving.

The combinations of particular information-processing and perceiving styles create learning style preferences: Diverger, Assimilator, Converger, and Accommodator. The presence of all four learning preferences in the classroom is a positive situation—this is an example of a time where difference is good and desired. Those individuals who have a minority learning style preference are vital to the effective functioning of the class.

Combining Perceiving and Processing: Kolb Learning Styles

- Divergers (high CE and RO)
- Assimilators (high RO and AC)
- Convergers (high AC and AE)
- Accommodators (high AE and CE)

Kolb Learning Styles
Diverger

- Divergers (Quadrant 1)
  - Integrate experience with own values
  - View learning environment from many perspectives
  - Are highly individualistic and seek to maximize personal choice
  - Like to ask "Why?"

Now the instructor discusses each of the learning styles. The following four slides describe the details of each learning style category. Each slide contains a characteristic question that often appeals to the natural curiosity of each learning style.

The qualities of the Diverger can be vital to the "kick off" of a team project. These individuals tend to promote inclusion of all team members and consideration of their ideas. This is especially useful during the team formation stage.

Assimilators will play an important role as team members begin to address the various tasks at hand. Because Assimilators tend to first think through an issue before taking action, teams staffed with Assimilators may demonstrate more depth than those without any. Assimilators often gravitate toward the theoretical or scientific aspects of the engineering curriculum. Many engineering professors are Assimilators because of their own natural proclivity toward the abstract which is then reinforced by their doctoral training and research.

**Kolb Learning Styles
Assimilator**

- Assimilators (Quadrant 2)
  - Integrate new experience with existing knowledge
  - Seek to make sense of the "big picture"
  - Develop/conceptualize models
  - Prefer deductive problem solving (general principles first, followed by details)
  - Like to ask "What?"

**Kolb Learning Styles
Converger**

- Convergers (Quadrant 3)
  - Integrate theory and practice by using abstract knowledge and common sense
  - Solve real problems with real constraints
  - Seek the solution, believing **one** to exist
  - Prefer to combine deductive and inductive reasoning skills
  - Like to ask "How?"

The Convergers will be integral team members when the time comes to begin narrowing solutions because they are drawn to the application of theory in service of practical outcomes or products.

Convergers excel at developing criteria and constraints against which solution alternatives can be evaluated. They are more compelled by empirical evidence when making design and team decisions than the opinions of their teammates. Teams comprised of multiple Convergers may develop into advocates for different empirically supported ideas resulting in intellectual conflict.

Accommodators will make vital contributions to the team endeavor by ensuring that various courses of action are explored. They are risk takers and are interested in innovative options and solutions that are outside the traditional engineering experience.

These individuals may enjoy the group aspects of teamwork and interacting with individuals. In addition, their strengths may include identifying and locating resources for an outside project via networking and investigating information and options beyond engineering.

**Kolb Learning Styles
Accomodator**

- Accommodators (Quadrant 4)
  - Integrate experience into application – often immediately
  - Are excited by challenging problems and new situations
  - Prefer inductive problem solving (generalize from specific examples to general principles)
  - Often learn by trial and error
  - Like to ask "What if?"

Each of us has a preferred learning style. Knowing that style and its strengths can assist us in structuring our learning of new material. In the same way, knowing the strengths of other styles can guide us in trying out new ways of learning.

Activity: Kolb in teams

Divide the class into groups with similar learning styles for further exploration of how learning styles can influence individual perceptions and comfort zones. The instructor should not be surprised if the class is not evenly divided among the four types, or is even missing a type.

This material encourages critical thought regarding learning style preferences and should lead students to consider how individual differences will contribute to a successfully working team. This section will resonate with Convergers, who are driven to learn by asking the question, "how?"

Kolb Learning Styles: Exercise

- Break into small groups with the same learning style
- Describe how you would like to learn material on… (topic to be supplied by instructor)
- Have one member of each team report the results of their discussion to the entire class

Preferred Learning Activity
(Record Team Answers and Discuss)

ACCOMMODATORS	DIVERGERS
CONVERGERS	ASSIMILATORS

Another activity asks students to describe how they would like a course instructor to teach material on a particular topic based on different learning styles. For example, query each learning style group, "how would you best learn new material on gravity, beam stress, etc?" Ask a recorder from each group to write the descriptions on the board (or on the PowerPoint® slide) and process the material with the entire class. As a result, the students should see differences by learning style. The groups will provide their observations of the different preferences by type… what do they see? Most students will be struck with the fact that some of their classmates are so different.

 Each learning style has *very* different expectations about teachers and the teachers' responsibilities for helping students learn. These differences in perception impact how students view their team experience as well.

Have a discussion on ways to use the knowledge gained from this module. This section's format will appeal to the accommodators in class, who are driven to learn by asking the question, "what if?"

Ask students to reflect on a time they had difficulty learning a particular subject and recall what steps they took to learn the material. What if they had known about their Kolb Learning Styles: how might that have made a difference? Could they have asked their instructor for more helpful guidance? Share reactions to exercise at beginning of next class session.

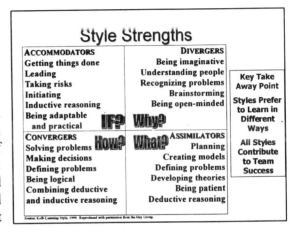

Style Strengths

ACCOMMODATORS	DIVERGERS	Key Take Away Point
Getting things done	Being imaginative	
Leading	Understanding people	
Taking risks	Recognizing problems	Styles Prefer
Initiating	Brainstorming	to Learn in
Inductive reasoning	Being open-minded	Different
Being adaptable and practical	IF? Why?	Ways
CONVERGERS	ASSIMILATORS	All Styles
Solving problems	How? What? Planning	Contribute
Making decisions	Creating models	to Team
Defining problems	Defining problems	Success
Being logical	Developing theories	
Combining deductive and inductive reasoning	Being patient Deductive reasoning	

Source: Kolb Learning Style, 1999. Reproduced with permission from the Hay Group.

Most engineering instructors tend to be Assimilators. This means that they present material in an abstract, theoretical fashion. Since most engineering students are Convergers, there can be a natural mismatch. An awareness of this issue can circumvent communication and teaching/learning difficulties.

Wrap Up: We Are Not All Alike
– Awareness of your strengths is vital for full team participation
– Don't confuse style differences with performance level differences
– Professionalism demands a focus on outcomes, not style
– Successful teams use the different skills of *all* members

The instructor should end on a positive note, emphasizing the valuable contribution each learning style makes to successful team functioning. Remind the students that the complete learning cycle requires the strengths and perspectives of all learning style types Understanding learning styles can enable students to "look at the big picture" when they encounter new material, instead of feeling frustrated at a perceived lack of clarity in an assignment.

The following slide summarizes the key ingredients for a successful team project, according to BESTEAMS. The instructor may wish to review and modify this list depending on personal preferences and team goals.

This material may be further tailored by the instructor based on the suggestions provided at the end of this MIP entitled "Class Adaptation Strategies."

Ingredients for a Successful Team

- Clarity of team goals and objectives
- Defined member roles and expectations
- Clear communication
- Productive team behaviors
- Awareness of group process, including learning style differences
- Professionalism in all interactions

Delivery Plan for Part II:

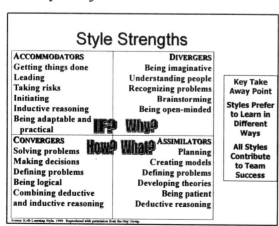

Designed for a 90-minute class period

This expanded section encourages students to use their newfound awareness of learning style to create a deeper understanding of team processes. It includes the following exercises 1) forming a team from a learning style point of view, 2) considering the "type" of the entire team, 3) evaluating the team's potential strengths and weaknesses.

A slide is provided that assists the instructor in reminding the students of the various style strengths.

Team formation

Show students the slide on the different learning styles. This may be a review if some time as elapsed since completing or working with the LSI. Remind them that different learning preferences have different strengths. Subsequently, an awareness of all styles is necessary.

Team Formation: Different Styles

You are a team finishing a class project. Your instructor is preparing for the next semester and asks you to make a recommendation on how teams should be formed in future classes based on your knowledge of learning styles.

Break into groups by learning style preference to discuss and report.

Activity: Using Learning Styles to Form Teams

Break students into small groups and ask them to answer the question on the accompanying slide: "How should teams be formed when taking into consideration Learning Style preferences?" Students can either enter their answers onto the PowerPoint® presentation, or write them on large sheets of paper to then share with the class.

This exercise allows students to (re)familiarize themselves with the material, as well as consider an extremely useful question.

Typical answers for this activity are provided in the slide and offer an appropriate starting point for class discussion. The instructor may need to push students to consider why knowing this information is important, particularly if the class is comprised of younger students who have had less experience working with teams.

This introduction provides the foundation for the next activity, where the focus is on the "team type" rather than notions of individual style preferences.

Expected Behavior in Teams
(Typical Answers)

	ACCOMMODATING	DIVERGING
Advising Instructor on Team Formation Methods	Prefer informal method Let each member choose Ask professor to discuss team roles first	Consider demographics Include student perspective Develop a process that is optimized for the individual
	CONVERGING	**ASSIMILATING**
	Collect data on skills needed Collect data on skill sets of students Create the best teams (make it an equation)	Set criteria for creating balanced teams Balance by GPA's of members Collect info on students Optimize process for task

---

 Understanding how to use individual differences to affect team formation and performance is an important component of sophisticated team functioning.

Identifying Team Learning Style

Team Learning Styles

Is your team predominately one style?
– For example:
  • Converging teams focus on the technical solution to the problem
  • Assimilating teams focus on the principles underlying the problem
  • Diverging teams focus on idea generation
  • Accommodating teams focus on the practical aspects of completing the project

Activity: Through lecture or question and answer, demonstrate the ways that different learning styles show up in team actions. In their project teams, ask students to discuss how their team performs and determine if there is a predominant style (based on a majority Kolb type or dominant members). Ask students for the positives and negatives of their team composition and introduce the idea that teams themselves have learning styles.

This section encourages students to think of teams as something more than a group of individuals, and asks them to consider how the team can be a more effective vehicle for project completion.

An awareness of the way your team "prefers" to function is vital when working toward project improvement and completion. Also, awareness of "what is missing" from your team in terms of Kolb preferences can help when team progress lags.

Organizing Your Team to Address Its Learning Style

Consider your team's predominant learning style. What are its strengths and weaknesses?
Some categories to consider are:
  – Planning and organizing
  – Communication frequency and openness
  – Decision making
  – Creativity
  – Conflict management
  – Technical mastery and attention to detail

Maximizing strengths and minimizing weaknesses

This section asks the teams to organize in a way that will take advantage of team strengths and minimize team weaknesses. For example, if the predominant team style is Converging, the team strengths may include decision making and technical mastery and its weakness by in the area of communication.

After teams have identified strengths and weaknesses, ask them to organize the team to address the weaknesses.

Depending on the predominant team style, the identified weaknesses will vary. For instance, if the team challenge is a poor record of task completion, the team may enact a better reporting system. If inefficient meetings are the problem, making sure team members have an agenda outlined before the next meeting may over come the obstacle.

Organizing Your Team

What must you include in your team's organization to promote your strengths and protect against the weaknesses?
  – Improve scheduling
  – Clarify roles
  – Design communication strategies
  – Other ?

Summary

- Your individual learning style informs the way you learn and the way you act in a team. The learning style itself is neither right nor wrong
- A successful team takes advantage of every member's learning style
- Teams can have a style of their own
- It is possible to organize the team to enhance its strengths and minimize its weaknesses

Summary and Wrap-Up

Working to prevent problems by analyzing team strengths and weaknesses, rather than being forced to respond to them, especially when time is short, will result in a smoother team experience. Understanding the way that Kolb's theory helps inform team interaction is summarized in the slide at the left. Additional considerations for wrapping up the class will depend on the class size, content, and classroom culture. See "Class Adaptation Strategies" at the end of this MIP.

Teaching to the Learning Styles: Personal Knowledge

CONVERGERS

Completing Kolb's learning styles inventory: The act of determining the scores and identifying the types will appeal to Convergers, who are driven to get a specific single answer or number. Convergers will argue with the instructor about whether the answer makes sense.

Kolb in teams activities: These exercises in learning style groups will resonate with Convergers, who like to specify how they wish to learn and how they want the course to be run.

Maximizing strengths and minimizing weaknesses: This activity identifies specific ways the team will be organized as well as the rules for member behavior. These exercises appeal to the Converger's desire for a specific answer or guideline.

DIVERGERS

Introduction to learning styles/Higher level questions: This activity appeals to the Diverger, who is interested in the reasons for doing something and seeing how the activity can be beneficial to the members of the team.

Sharing personal experience: When the instructor shares a personal experience that demonstrates the value of self-knowledge, this appeals to the Diverger's sense of the long-term benefits to individuals and prevents the discomfort they have with insensitive teachers.

Team formation activity: Looking at multiple problem solving options appeals to the Diverger. Likewise, being aware of the ideas and feelings of others allows them to see the issue from multiple perspectives.

ASSIMILATORS

Introducing learning objectives: When the instructor outlines the merits of learning styles in the team environment, Assimilators become clear about the long term value of their learning.

Formal lecture on Kolb: This activity gives students the general concepts and broad background about learning styles, thereby helping them understand the "big picture." This perspective is attractive to Assimilators, who want to understand the theory before specific application. Furthermore, this material helps students see the need for creating teams with different learning styles.

Identifying team learning style: This activity provides an overall conceptual picture of the nature of team functioning. Subsequently, this information allows Assimilators to understand why the team acts in specific ways.

ACCOMMODATORS

Class discussion on style strengths: This activity helps to make sense of what was learned and put it to use. Specifically, the section's format will appeal to the Accommodators in the class, since it helps explain why they have had difficulties with teammates in the past and suggests ways to resolve these conflicts.

Team formation activity: This exercise allows students practice the ideas presented. Since Accommodators prefer to learn by trial and error, they will appreciate this opportunity.

Class Adaptation Strategies

A. *Size:* In larger size classes, give completion of the LSI as a homework assignment and ask students to bring the scored instrument back to class. Assign sections of seats to each learning style and have students directly take seats in those sections for the exercises. Alternatively, some exercises might be completed individually by having students write down their thoughts and then share them with the people seated close by.

B. *Content:* Link the notion of learning styles to specific aspects of course content if possible. For example, if the course involves a project such as building a submarine, robot, or highway construction, ask which learning styles types are likely to prefer being involved with specific aspects of the projects. For example, accommodators might be more interested in the "human" factors or marketing aspects of the project while the Assimilators would like to work on the science aspects such as increasing fuel efficiency. In turn, the Convergers might prefer designing and building alternative power shaft components and the Divergers might like to work on the overall plan for completing the project.

C. *Classroom Culture:* Depending on academic culture, individual differences may be accentuated or minimized. Kolb preferences are independent of race and gender and independent of team role (leader, follow-through person, etc.): reminding students of this fact may encourage them to keep an open mind regarding this material. All types can play all roles. Incorporating this understanding into the classroom culture should encourage students to create an open, trusting environment.

 Individual differences are an important aspect of innovative team functioning, for variety contributes to the creativity and success of team activities.

Follow-Up Materials

A. *Homework:* Reading assignment. Instructor choice (see Kolb references at the end of "Theoretical Foundations" and "Personal Awareness References" in section 3.6). Depending on the class level, the appropriate reading will differ.

B. *Homework:* Reflective writing assignment or journal entry. Ask students to respond to questions such as: "Do you see your own learning style preferences at work in how you approach your tasks in this course? What one activity could you try that is the opposite of how you normally learn something? Try it and comment on how it felt to learn that way." Although traditional engineering students may resist this type of activity, tying theory to practice has been shown to improve cognitive learning processes.

C. *Classroom Follow-Up:* At the beginning of next class, ask for volunteers to read their journal entries or reflections aloud. If posted electronically to the instructor, have the instructor read anonymous entries and discuss with the class. When possible, instructors should note if learning activities are especially appropriate to a specific Kolb style in order to increase students' appreciation that "teaching around the cycle" is occurring.

D. *Exam or quiz items:* Add questions such as the following to course quizzes or tests: "What strengths does your learning style give you for understanding the course material?" or "What suggestions can you make to me, the course instructor, on how to communicate information on <insert a specific topic covered in your course> to someone with your learning style and habits? Please explain why this method would be useful to you." By assessing this material, you are placing a tangible value on the material covered in this module.

Due to the cost of the Kolb Learning Style Inventory (LSI), BESTEAMS recommends contacting your school bookstore to order the LSIs from the Hay Group. Students may then purchase a copy as one of the required "texts" for the class. Included in the packet is a thorough booklet on Kolb's Learning Style Inventory and the instrument itself. The material included in the Kolb packet can be assigned for homework. In addition, the booklet includes useful information on how learning style has been linked to careers and other behaviors of interest to students. Please note that this material makes clear the dominance of Convergers in engineering; this might be discouraging or intimating to non-Convergers in the classroom. The instructor should reiterate that all types are needed and important to the field of engineering, despite the fact that some learners gravitate to the area.

Source for Purchasing Kolb Learning Style Inventory Test Materials
The Hay Group/TRG
116 Huntington Ave.
Fourth Floor
Boston, MA 02116

http://trgmcber.haygroup.com/Products/learning
Phone: 800.729.8074
Fax: 617.927.5060

3.6 Personal Awareness for Students: References

Desjardins, C. (1989). The meaning of Gilligan's concept of *Different Voice* for the learning environment. In C.S. Pearson, D.L. Shavlik, & J.G. Touchton (Eds.), *Educating the majority: Women challenge tradition in higher education* (pp. 121-133). New York: MacMillan Publishing.

Felder, R.M., Silverman, L.K. (1998). Learning and teaching styles in engineering education. *Engineering Education 78*(7), 674-681.

Gibbs, G. (1997). *Learning in teams: A student manual,* (2nd ed.). Oxford Press.

Guys-Sheftall, B., & Bell-Scott, P. (1989). A view from the margin. In C.S. Pearson, D.L. Shavlik, & J.G. Touchton (Eds.), *Educating the majority: Women challenge tradition in higher education* (pp. 205-218). New York: MacMillan Publishing.

Kolb, D.A. (1999). *The Kolb Learning Style Inventory (ver. 3).* Boston: Hay Group.

McIntosh, P.M. (1989). Curricular re-vision: The new knowledge for a new age. In C.S. Pearson, D.L. Shavlik, & J.G. Touchton (Eds.), *Educating the majority: Women challenge tradition in higher education* (pp. 400-412). New York: MacMillan Publishing.

Mead, P.F., Moore, D., Natishan, M., Schmidt, L., Goswami, I., Brown, S., et al. (1999). Faculty and student views on engineering student team effectiveness. *Journal of Women and Minorities in Science and Engineering*, 5, 351-363.

Peterson, G. (1998, June). ABET Engineering Criteria 2000, Keynote address, 1998 WEPAN National Conference, Seattle, WA.

Rosser, S. V. (1997). *Re-engineering female friendly science.* New York: Teachers College Press.

Wilde, D. (1997). Using team preferences to guide design team composition. *Proceedings of DETC '97, 1997 ASME Design Engineering Technical Conference*, Sept. 14-17, DETC97/DTM-3890.

Chapter 4 BESTEAMS MODULE INTERPERSONAL EFECTIVENESS

4.1 Introduction to Module

This Module Implementation Plan (MIP) is the second educational component of the Introductory BESTEAMS curricular initiative. It builds on the Kolb learning style theoretical foundations laid in the Introductory Personal Knowledge MIP; as such, specific elements are included that refer to that material. If an instructor chooses to teach this module to students who have not experienced the Kolb Personal Knowledge information, some material covered in the 90 minute extended version of this module may have to be omitted. While the module is designed to stand alone, there is some advantage to teaching the earlier information, thus initiating students to the idea of individual difference on teams and helping them progress from one module to the next.

In this module, emphasis is placed on learning to function collaboratively and productively within teams. The material was chosen for its importance in team functioning: there is no team that is all task and no process. The module covers three aspects of team process critical to successful team performance, including the basic stages of team development, giving and receiving feedback to the members on the team, and idea generating tools, including verbal and written brainstorming. The latter techniques are introduced in this module because one common source of interpersonal strain in teams is the variety of view points and the difficulty in making a decision when everyone disagrees.

Once again, the longer version of this module utilizes the Kolb LSI as an attribute filter, reminding students that personal awareness is a first step in developing a productive team. If students do not remember their Learning Style Inventory (LSI) results, or if the class members did not complete the first module, instructors can provide a brief lecture on Kolb's theory, encouraging students to consider the role that learning style preference might play in their own learning as well as working together on a team.

4.2 Team Functioning: Theoretical Foundations

Tuckman's Model

When academics, lay people, business trainers, and other experts in team development speak of the stages of group functioning, they are commonly referring to Bruce Tuckman's classic 1965 article, "Developmental Sequence in Small Groups." Based on a review of available literature, Tuckman developed his "forming, storming, norming, performing" theory, in which he determined four sequential and predictable phases group members experience as they work together. In 1977, he added a fifth stage, "adjourning," to describe the project completion phase (see figure 4.1). Although Tuckman himself credits some of the popularity of his theory to its "quotability," the accuracy of his work has withstood the test of time with those in the team training world (Tuckman, 2001, p. 384; Runkel, 1971).

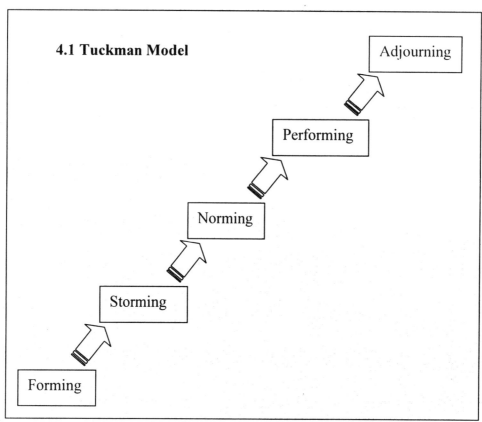

4.1 Tuckman Model

Adapted from JISC Info Net, 2004

The first stage of team development, "forming," is characterized by a period of time where students "test" each other to determine which behaviors are acceptable in the team. Often one student will be identified as the leader in this stage, and the others will look to him or her for guidance. During this phase, the task may seem ambiguous to students, resulting in numerous attempts to clarify the objective through questioning the appointed leader and/or the instructor. The strengths and weaknesses of group members begin to emerge, signifying the readiness to move into the next stage: storming.

"Storming" is what many students think of when they consider teamwork: active conflict. Tuckman (2001) writes, "The lack of unity is an outstanding feature of this phase" (p. 387). The key is to prepare students for this stage by teaching that it is a predictable part of virtually all team experiences. As team members struggle to remain individuals within the team and yet work together on projects that require collaborative effort, hostility toward one another can be manifested. This module provides information on giving and receiving feedback, abilities especially important when tempers flare and project completion seems impossible.

The third stage, "norming," occurs when students begin to reconcile individual versus team desires. At this point, team members accept the team and those within it, which in turn allows group cohesion. Roles and responsibilities are better understood and agreed upon. Tuckman explains that positive personal feelings may begin to emerge in this stage, and others have noted that a sense of personal accomplishment often arises (Page & Donelan, 2003). Teams that have reached this point are productive and accomplish their tasks with little or no conflict.

In the fourth stage, "performing," the team becomes a "problem-solving instrument" (Tuckman, 1965, p. 70). Members know the overarching goals and are moving directly toward them in a deliberate way. Page and Donelan (2003) characterize this stage as one filled with positive energy: team members trust each other and enjoy working together. Humor emerges once the team has established its interpersonal norms. The goal and the end of the project are in sight.

Tuckman and collaborator Mary Ann Jensen added the fifth stage, "adjourning" in 1977, after a review of 22 new studies indicated the existence of a coherent post-project completion team interaction. Essentially, this stage refers to the break-up of the group, and a movement away from the initial four stages toward closure—both personally and in terms of the project itself. Hopefully students experience satisfaction regarding the completion of the task; however, some may feel insecurity as they realize the future requires finishing tasks without their experienced and trusted teammates. The adjourning stage is an often overlooked time for directed reflection. Encouraging students to review the ways their group worked well together, as well as how they clashed, will allow them to better understand team processes in the future. Moreover, being able to think back on the roles and tasks they particularly liked and disliked will help students better appreciate their own strengths and weaknesses related to engineering project teams.

Constructive Feedback

Although Tuckman's five stages of team development have been well-documented, there are "tricks of the trade" that will assist students in moving from one stage to the next. Giving and receiving feedback is a vital skill for members of a team to possess, and encourages healthy team development. Some guidelines for constructive feedback are provided in the following section. Adapted from *The Team Handbook* (1988), by Peter R. Scholtes.

- Affirm the importance of feedback: Feedback is imperative to the team that wishes to correct its negative behaviors and strengthen its positive characteristics. Without effective communication, team members lack the ability to self-monitor project progress. Becoming comfortable in giving and receiving feedback is one of the most essential skills a student learns from participating in a project team.

- Give both complimentary and constructive feedback: Feedback should not only be associated with telling someone "the bad news." While it may be easy to identify what is *not* working within a team, providing positive feedback should not be overlooked. Studies have shown that individuals respond more readily to criticism if it is delivered in conjunction with complimentary information (Brinko, 1993).

- Know the circumstances: Providing feedback is useless if respondents fail to explain the "who, what, when, where, and why" of the message. Focused feedback that provides concrete examples, as well as the actions that led to the criticism, will help the recipient understand how to better perform in the future.

- Choose the time and place for feedback delivery: Depending on the type of feedback, different environments may be appropriate. In the business world, it is recommended that feedback be delivered privately (Thompson & Sligar, 1999). In the student team setting, however, it may be useful to provide positive and negative feedback with the entire team on a regular basis. Scholtes (1988) reminds us that, "Constructive feedback can only happen within a context of listening to and caring about the person" (p. 6-25). In other words, the feedback must be part of a larger conversation designed to help the team make changes and/or improvements. Remembering this rule of thumb ensures that the feedback is delivered in a thoughtful and deliberate way.

- Know how to give feedback: There are a number of ways to provide constructive feedback to team members. In her review of the subject, Brinko (1993) determined that, "feedback is more effective when conveyed in a variety of modes" (p. 579). Part of the team forming process may involve determining the ways in which individuals prefer to receive feedback; while one team member might prefer verbal feedback, another might like to receive such information in writing. Regardless of the mode, certain guidelines should be followed when giving feedback. Adapted from Scholtes, 1998.

  - Use desciptive language
  - Avoid using labels
  - Curb exaggerations
  - Refrain from being judgmental
  - Speak only for yourself, not others (unless designated as the spokesperson by the team)
  - Share your own perceptions first, instead of referring to the other person ("I feel…")
  - Speak in statements, not questions
  - Provide feedback on the facts, never conjecture
  - Give feedback about behaviors people can change
  - Assist others in hearing and accepting your positive compliments

- Know how to accept feedback: Because feedback is often delivered in the form of criticism, it may be difficult to accept. Scholtes (1988) recognizes that feedback is usually given by individuals who do not know the feedback guidelines described above. In this case, it may be up to the recipient to help the critic rephrase the feedback into a form that allows a productive conversation to occur. A question such as, "what did I say or do to dissatisfy you?" may place the dialogue back on track (Scholtes, 1988, p. 6-30). Even when mostly positive feedback in anticipated, Scholtes (1988) offers six recommendations for accepting feedback:

  - Breathe
  - Listen carefully
  - Ask questions for clarity
  - Acknowledge the feedback
  - Acknowledge valid points
  - Ask for the time you need to sort out what you have heard
      (From Scholtes, 1988, p. 6-30-6-31)

Ultimately, learning how to provide constructive feedback is an important step in developing teams that are able work together productively.

Brainstorming/"Brainwriting"

No matter how well-adjusted a team may be, certain strategies exist to help team members examine possibilities before acting, as well as respond to the occasional roadblocks. Advertising executive Alex Osborn coined the team "brainstorming" in the 1930s after noting his employees lacked creativity in problem solving (Panitz, 1998). Osborn's solution was to develop a technique in which individuals would generate as many solutions to a problem as possible, reserving judgment on all suggestions until the activity was completed. Brainstorming can be a useful tool for increasing options before winnowing them to the final decision. Engineering instructors have noted that "brainstorming's power lies in its emphasis on keeping an open mind and proposing a multitude of suggestions," characteristics that are sometimes lacking predominantly Converging teams (Panitz, 1998).

Brainstorming Session Guidelines

- Assist everyone in allowing their ideas to flow freely, ignoring any instinct to move in a strict linear fashion. The more ideas the better.
- Avoid discussion during the brainstorming session. There will be time for that later.
- No prejudgment during session. No criticizing of another's ideas, not even with an eye roll or a chuckle!
- Encourage hitchhiking—the building-upon of ideas generated by others in the group
- Write every idea somewhere prominent so the whole group can easily scan the list

Adapted from Scholtes, 1988

In addition, Panitz (1998) shares the recommendations that other engineering educators have made:

- Carefully define the problem from the beginning. Identifying the task up-front allows participants to ensure they are generating solutions to the right problem.

- Take some time for individuals to consider the problem before the group tackles it. There should be at least a couple minutes of private reflection before the brainstorming activity begins.

- Create a comfortable environment so that even silly ideas can be presented.

- Appoint a group facilitator to make certain that the group follows all rules of brainstorming and keeps track of the ideas.

Much research has been performed on the role of brainstorming in project completion. Some experimental research has appeared to indicate a "productivity loss" that can come with brainstorming, as the activity requires much collaborative time from the team and does not necessarily produce a greater number of ideas than the individuals could have developed on their own. However, Sutton and Hargadon (1996) are swift to point out that brainstorming success should not be judged solely on the number of ideas generated. Instead, successful completion of tasks using creative methods and skill variety among members should be among the criteria when determining success. This is particularly true when considering brainstorming within the engineering classroom context.

Students will have differing comfort levels regarding speaking out. This can be particularly true when considering members of under-represented groups in the classroom, who may be reluctant to draw attention to themselves. In addition, some students may feel vulnerable or exposed and want to avoid "saying something stupid." In situations such as these, a form of written brainstorming can be used. Called "brainwriting," its advantage is that vocal group members cannot overwhelm the contributions of quieter teammates (Shirley Poertner, as cited in Panitz, 1998). The rules for brainwriting are generally agreed upon and are similar to those in brainstorming.

Brainwriting Procedure

1. Participants identify the problem to be addressed. Whether brainstorming or brainwriting, this step ensures focused attention on the upcoming task.

2. Participants *write down* answers to the problem on a piece of paper. Teams may use this step to work on multiple dimensions of the problem simultaneously, with each sheet of paper representing a certain aspect.

3. After a previously agreed-upon period of time, participants pass their paper to a neighbor.

4. The neighbor builds on those solutions, writing his or her new suggestions on the same piece of paper before passing to the subsequent person.

5. This continues until no longer productive, usually three to five "rounds," depending on the size of the group.

6. Participants read ideas aloud and analyze them. By the end of the brainwriting session, teams should have a short-list of the most viable solutions to the identified problem.

Whether brainstorming or brainwriting is preferred, the eventual evaluation of the ideas is vital to successful incorporation into a team project. Donald Woods writes, "85 to 95 percent of the ideas will be real junk, but hidden in those junky ideas will be something really revolutionary" (as cited in Panitz, 1998). Reminding students of this fact may be useful as they work to pare down the number of solutions they developed.

Paring down ideas generated from brainstorming or brainwriting involves a different set of tools. The goal of these activities, often called "decision making tools," is to help team members evaluate the strength and weaknesses of the various ideas. Among the most common are force field analysis and multi-voting techniques. These techniques differ in terms of complexity and the degree of analysis that results and provide students with other skills to enhance their interpersonal effectiveness. For more information see Section 4.3: Sources Cited.

Learning how to work with one another can be a complicated and stressful process. However, this skill is a vital addition to engineering students' knowledge portfolios. Although ABET requirements lend immediate motivation for adding this material to engineering curricula, engineers must learn how to get along with others and maximize everyone's contribution to team goals in order to function successfully in today's industry. While students do not always need to agree with their teammates, learning how to disagree constructively is a lifelong skill. This module provides the engineering educator with an introduction to key interpersonal team skills.

4.3 Sources Cited

Brinko, K. (1993). The practice of giving feedback to improve teaching: What is effective? *The Journal of Higher Education, 64*(5), 574-593.

JISC Info Net. (2004). *Tuckman model pic.* Retrieved June 20, 2004 from
http://www.jiscinfonet.ac.uk/InfoKits/infokit-related-files/tuckman-model-pic

Page, D., & Donelan, J.G. (2003). Team-building tools for students. *Journal of Education for Business, 78*(3), 125-128.

Panitz, B. (1998, March). Brain storms. *ASEE Prism, 7,* 24-29.

Runkel, P.J. (1971). Stages of group development: An empirical test of Tuckman's hypothesis. *Journal of Applied Behavioral Science, 7*(2), 180-193.

Scholtes, P.R. (1988). *The team handbook: How to use teams to improve quality.* Madison, WI: Joiner Associated, Inc.

Thompson, C.B., & Sligar, S. (1999). *Constructive feedback is good!* Training Systems, Inc. Retrieved November 14, 2003 from http://www.trainingsys.com/articles/consfdck.html

Tuckman, B.W. (1965). Developmental sequence in small groups. *Psychological Bulletin, 63*(6), 384-399.

Tuckman, B.W. (2001, Spring). Author's note. *Group Facilitation: A Research and Applications Journal, 3,* 66-81.

4.4 50-Minute Class Overview: Working Effectively Within Teams
Interpersonal Knowledge

Module Outline
- Introduce objectives of lesson
- Ask broad questions to generate discussion
- Deliver formal lecture on team-development theory
- Ensure students practice giving and receiving feedback in groups
- Initiate class discussion: How should teams brainstorm their ideas?
- Facilitate brainstorming and "brainwriting" in groups

Expected Student Outcomes
- Insight into working on teams through examining team formation and team processes
- Insight into the connections between clear communication in teams and healthy team dynamics
- Insight into brainstorming methods that increase team productivity

Assessment/Homework Options
- Add questions in midterm or final exam
- Assign teamwork reading assignment: instructor choice
- Assign reflective writing assignment

Materials Needed
- PowerPoint Slides
- Computer
- Projector
- Large sheets of paper for groups
- Markers to use for writing on paper

90-Minute Class Overview: Extended Class Outline & Additional Outcomes

Extended Class Outline
- Review the Kolb Learning Styles material, emphasizing how this knowledge can improve "process" skills
- Using process skills in teams: writing "how to" instructions
- Practicing brainstorming/brainwriting in teams

Additional Expected Outcomes
- Insight into the ways in which interpersonal dynamics affect teamwork
- Insight into giving and receiving feedback within teams
- Insight into maximizing team effectiveness when dealing with different learning styles

4.5 BESTEAMS Module Implementation Plan (MIP)
Introductory Level Interpersonal Effectiveness

Topic: *Working Effectively Within Teams*

Tracks	Personal Knowledge	Interpersonal Effectiveness	Project Management
Introductory	Kolb Learning Styles	Team Development & Communications Basics	Managing Your Project: Planning & Time

Introduction/Motivation

This module addresses several key aspects of *interpersonal functioning* within student project teams. Specifically, students will learn three areas of knowledge fundamental to successful teams: knowledge of typical stages of team development; giving and receiving feedback, with emphasis on developing good listening skills; and tools for generating new ideas in teams, including brainstorming strategies.

For students who have already been trained in the Kolb Learning Style Index (LSI), the additional training section outlines uses of their knowledge of Kolb learning styles in the context of team dynamics. Because individual learning style preferences are integral to the BESTEAMS model, the MIP is organized so that each learning style preference is addressed: Diverging, Assimilating, Converging, and Accommodating. By adapting materials and the presentation to "teach around the cycle," instructors encourage their students to "learn around the cycle."

The complete PowerPoint® presentation shown in this module is available for download at **http://www.enme.umd.edu/labs/BESTEAMS/**

Expected Outcomes

Upon implementation of this module, students should experience numerous outcomes that facilitate the development of useful team skills, including:

Module Part I

- Insight into team formation and team processes
- Insight into making connections between clear communication in teams and healthy team dynamics
- Insight into brainstorming methods that increase team productivity

Module Part II

- Insight into the ways interpersonal dynamics affect teamwork
- Insight into giving and receiving feedback within teams
- Insight into maximizing team effectiveness when dealing with different learning styles

Delivery Plan Part I: Designed for a 50-minute class period

Interpersonal Effectiveness Learning Objectives

- Appreciate group dynamics and their impact on team performance
- Understand basic stages of group development in teams
- Practice basic communication skills (e.g., active listening, giving and receiving feedback)
- Learn brainstorming techniques to increase team productivity

---

Introduce the module and the objectives of the session. Class characteristics should be considered when determining how best to present the expected outcomes of the module. The underlying course in which this module is presented provides a framework for the type of communication and interaction that will ensue. For example, in a design project course it is natural to have an idea generation phase when all members of the team are encouraged to describe alternatives, even outlandish ones. At this stage, communication should support engagement and creativity.

Why Focus on Teams?

- Teams allow us to offer a more balanced product (remember Kolb)
- Teams improve effectiveness by helping to minimize personal weaknesses and utilize individual strengths
- Teams encourage students to become effective problem solvers– a vital skill in "the real world"

Introduction to Interpersonal Effectiveness

Begin discussion on the role of teamwork in engineering education. Reiterate that these process skills are vital for individuals who want to work in industry, for teamwork is a reality in engineering professions. This section is designed to encourage reflection about why the ability to work together is necessary in today's engineering workplaces and classrooms. The structure of the learning activities should particularly resonate with Divergers, who are driven to learn by asking the question, "why?"

The Socratic Method is one teaching style frequently used when teaching this material and involves asking students probing questions, rather than simply providing them with answers. This process encourages students to think critically in a disciplined and logical way.

Ask higher level, Socratic questions of the students. Questions could include:

- Why has teamwork become the most common means of engineering practice?
- Why do some students dislike participation in student project teams?

 A group project involves individuals working together to achieve the same outcome, such as solving a homework problem. A team project involves individuals working together to produce an outcome larger and more complex than an individual could produce alone.

Sharing personal experience

For this activity, the instructor relates a personal experience that illustrates why teamwork and its accompanying skills are important to successful functioning as an engineer. An example taken from experience with industry, such as consulting with a product development team, or from working with other faculty members, such as designing a clean room, may prove useful. This emphasizes the importance of teamwork in the professional world.

 Possessing the ability to function with a diverse group of individuals on a project team is critical in today's engineering professions. As team projects became more complicated, interpersonal effectiveness becomes vital to successful project completion.

Formal lecture from instructor

This section serves to place teamwork theory in a formal educational context. Assimilators will particularly appreciate this activity, as they learn by asking the question, "what?" Resources for this lecture include PowerPoint® presentation slides
(available at **http://www.enme.umd.edu/labs/BESTEAMS/**) and background information provided in this section. For more information, see Team Formation and Communication References in Section 4.6.

Typical Stages of Team Development

- Forming
- Storming
- Norming
- Performing
- Adjourning/Completing

Team development begins with information on the stages of team development: forming, storming, norming, performing, and adjourning. All teams, regardless of age, education level, or purpose, experience these stages of team formation. However, this process may be particularly anxiety-provoking for students engaged in teamwork. Students may not anticipate a phase of resistance to progress and interpersonal tension as necessary during mature team development. Discussing team development processes removes some of the mystery of teamwork, and will allow for less stressful team experiences.

Forming: Ask students questions designed to help them recall their previous team experiences. Questions to use may include. How have instructors designed the teams you have been on? Did the process work? Why or why not? What initial activities took place to help the team form? These questions focus team members on the logistics required for their project completion as well as identifying skills needed at different points throughout the term. At this point, students may be displaying their "best" team skills as they choose the appropriate interpersonal behaviors.

Characteristics of Forming

The team is figuring out the task ahead and individuals are becoming acquainted

- Typical Feelings: Excitement, pride in participation, anxiety about unknowns ahead
- Typical Behaviors: Attempts to determine acceptable behaviors, how to deal with problems, identify roles in the group

Characteristics of Storming

The team feels everything seems to be falling apart; group is demoralized by the task

- Typical Feelings: Resistance to trying new approaches, emotional highs and lows, worry about workload
- Typical Behaviors: Arguing, blaming instructor for unrealistic expectations, competition

Storming: Every team has a phase of ups and downs when members are first learning to operate together. It can be clumsy as team members discover strengths and challenges of the project and of the team members themselves.

The instructor should tell students that storming is an inevitable, but not necessarily cataclysmic, part of developing an effective team. A storming period may proceed the deadline for the team's first deliverable. While uncomfortable, the results of this stage include greater clarity of purpose, better understanding of team roles and expectations, and the bonding that occurs after facing a common challenge. Early deadlines and feedback can "provoke" the crisis of storming since they push the team to get moving. Asking for peer feedback may also bring on storming as individuals must evaluate the actions of others.

Norming: After completing the storming phase, the most successful teams take time to reflect. While some instructors require that teams create a contract or group charter before working together, this is a good time to review or renegotiate team and project expectations. Instructors can encourage advancing to, and getting past, storming by setting early deadlines and providing feedback on deliverables. Norming results in a stronger team identity, a refreshed commitment to the task at hand, and a more sophisticated approach to giving and receiving feedback.

Characteristics of Norming

The team comes together and adapts to ground rules; emotional conflict is reduced

- Typical Feelings: Sense of team cohesion and pride; relief that task is going to be completed after all
- Typical Behaviors: Greater collaboration and sharing among members, smoother team functioning, ability to use feedback constructively

Characteristics of Performing

The team recognizes its strengths and overcomes weaknesses to accomplish the task

- Typical Feelings: Insight into group processes, satisfaction with team's progress, close attachment to team members
- Typical Behaviors: Ability of members to self correct and prevent or work through group issues

Performing: Inexperienced students may expect their teams to advance to the performing stage on the first day of class. This stage, with its efficient approach to project tasks, is what most engineering students think of as teamwork. Introducing students to predictable stages of team development can greatly relieve their stress concerning what appears to be initial poor team performance during the necessary forming and storming phases. The most important observation for students to take from this module may be that performing, with its positive feelings and accomplishments, is the result of prior stages in the team's development.

Adjourning: This is an often overlooked opportunity for directed reflection. In typical engineering project teams, students present their work and complete written reports during the last week of class. While the project task maybe be concluded with these verbal and written summaries, the team interpersonal processes (including what each student has learned) are often overlooked in the end of the semester rush.

If the instructor can set aside some time for the team to look back over its most and least successful activities for the semester, students will more quickly appreciate their own contributions to the team, see the pattern of team development more clearly, and experience personal "closure" regarding the ending of this particular team effort.

Characteristics of Adjourning/Completing

The team gears down, occurs once the project nears completion

- Typical Feelings: Satisfaction, sadness at ending of group interaction, insights into personal abilities in terms of teamwork
- Typical Behaviors: Analyses of team strengths, weaknesses, history of project, what could be done differently to improve future projects

Activity: Group discussion

The instructor has students group together for discussion of the information presented in the lecture. Depending on the size of the class, this ensuing discussion may take different forms: the instructor may moderate a larger dialogue or small groups may report to their classmates after a period of interaction. Guiding questions are included on the accompanying slide. As students work with their groups, they ideally will recognize the stages of team development in their previous team experiences.

Group Discussion

- What have been your best and worst team experiences and why?
- How does understanding the stages of team development allow you to interpret why you felt that way about your team experiences?

Basic Communication Skills

- Giving and receiving constructive feedback
- Engaging in active listening

Continuation of instructor lecture: Communication

The stages of team formation are predictable and tools exist to help students and teams move past roadblocks. This section provides information on two key skills that facilitate successful interpersonal functioning on teams: the ability to give and receive feedback and the capacity to listen effectively. Everyday team interactions require communication skills. A fully-engaged team member will naturally participate in feedback and listening. Possessing fluency in these skills will promote complete team participation.

Effective Feedback: General Guidelines

- Remember to give POSITIVE **and** NEGATIVE feedback
- Understand the context: Put comments in a time/place/situation (vs. "you always....")
- Determine if the person is receptive to feedback

Feedback guidelines: There are times when a formal member-to-team member feedback process should be undertaken, such as after receiving instructor evaluation of a major project milestone. At the beginning of this activity, students should acknowledge the importance of giving and receiving feedback, as well as how challenging this process may be for some team members. This is a skill that students will use throughout their education and take into their professional careers. As with any new skill, students' comfort level will increase as the techniques are practiced.

Feedback specifics: Learning to provide effective feedback is an important skill for each responsible and successful team member. The accompanying slides describe behaviors for effectively giving and receiving feedback. Some engineering students may be uncomfortable with the phrase "I feel," which initiates the feedback process. Though this vocabulary may be non-scientific, its use naturally leads the speaker to first reveal personal reactions and only then identify causal behaviors. For example, a student might say, "I feel embarrassed when the group report contains errors you missed during your assigned proofreading."

Giving Effective Feedback: Specifics

- Talk first about yourself ("I feel...") THEN others ("When you do....")
- Be descriptive and specific about actions, behaviors
- Do not use labels or exaggerate
- Restrict your feedback to things you know for certain (perhaps have checked out with other members of the team)
- Give feedback about behaviors people can change

Receiving Feedback

- Listen carefully (try to put defensiveness on hold)
- Ask questions for clarity
- Acknowledge valid points, recognize how people could have come to their conclusions (acknowledge the feedback)
- Take time to sort out what you heard
- Tell the person what you will do to change
- Ask for assistance or future feedback
- Say THANKS!

Gibbs, G. (1994).

Receiving feedback: Almost everyone is comfortable accepting positive feedback. Conversely, accepting negative feedback is a rare talent. Learning to do so will set students apart from their less-able peers, as well as teach team members how to recognize behaviors that are hindering their success. Furthermore, the ability to receive feedback is essential for lifelong learning. The guidelines on the accompanying slide encourage students to learn from their experiences as well as adopt a receptive attitude toward the perceptions of their teammates.

Steps to Good Listening

- Step 1: Once your attention is focused, listen carefully to the words being said (try to minimize internal distractions e.g., focusing on what YOU want to say next, daydreaming)

  If external distractions (e.g., noise, unpleasant surroundings) are too much, ask the speaker to wait until you can listen better

---

Steps to good listening: Today's technology allows continuous multi-tasking, often to the detriment of face-to-face communication. Truly effective listening requires focusing complete attention on the individual physically with you. In other words, the listeners must remove their hands from the computer keyboards or turn off their cellular phones. When using online technology for the team project, the same principles of focusing complete attention apply. For example, one should not open arriving email in the middle of an online dialogue.

Because of the culture that has developed, the gift of your full attention is perceived as a significant gesture. Paraphrasing reinforces that the listener is providing his or her full attention and allows the speaker to confirm that the right message has been communicated.

Attending skills are different based on the medium being used. Students may need to experiment with appropriate listening behaviors for interactions that are not "face-to-face." After the lecture, students are encouraged to practice what they have learned, working with each other to give and receive feedback.

Steps to Good Listening (cont'd)

- Step 2: Paraphrase what was said:
  - "what I hear you saying is…"
  - "as I understand it…"
  - "in other words…"
  - "so, you are saying…"

  Ask the speaker to repeat if you have misunderstood!

Practicing Team Communication Skills

- Break into triads
- Use the scenario provided to give and receive feedback
- Third member observes and provides feedback about the interaction

---

Activity: Practicing team communication skills

In this exercise, break class into groups of three and ask students to give and receive feedback to each other. The third member is the observer, whose job it is to offer suggestions and reactions to the interaction. It may be useful to provide a scenario for students to use, particularly one that is pertinent to the subject material. Sample feedback scenarios for instructors are provided in Appendix.

 The ability to work effectively on project teams requires a specific skill-set of communication practices and tools.

Introduction to brainstorming

The instructor introduces brainstorming strategies/techniques for idea generation/problem solutions, as discussed in the introduction to this section. Brainstorming is a key requirement for successful team functioning and can help prevent inaction as members scramble to decide what do to. Brainstorming builds interpersonal expertise because it encourages all students to participate, not just the most dominant team members. It also prevents premature closure of problem solving methods as well as the group going along with a self declared expert for lack of other options. Finally, brainstorming is also a project management skill because the process can assist a group that has reached an impasse or seems to be out of ideas.

Activity: Brainstorming strategies

Introduce ways to use brainstorming strategies. This will resonate with Convergers, who are driven to learn by answering the question "how?" Many students are familiar with brainstorming in general, but may not be familiar with specific techniques. Brainstorming is a common activity in projects and benefits from full participation of· all team members. To do it well does require some discipline, as those most comfortable sharing their ideas will need to rein in their enthusiasm. Likewise, those who are customarily quiet will need to push themselves to make use of these methods.

> ## Why Brainstorming?
>
> * Builds interpersonal expertise because all students participate
> * Quiets the "loudest talker" and prevents quick solutions
> * Develops a skill that is useful in project management

 A variety of solutions exist to ensure that all voices are heard within teams. Utilizing these techniques will improve team cohesion and product outcome.

Activities: Brainstorming and brainwriting

> ## Verbal Brainstorming: Procedure
>
> * Present a carefully defined problem
> * Appoint a facilitator to safeguard the process and a recorder to capture ideas
> * The recorder copies all suggestions on board/easel as they are named
> * Take a moment to think about the problem before addressing it verbally
> * Ground rules: no discussion, no reaction, no judgment

Brainstorming: Conduct a verbal brainstorming exercise with the entire class or among teams. Only 10 minutes are required if the ground rules are followed. This activity reinforces the value of the method when using the ground rules, and will particularly answer the learning needs of accommodators, who find meaning in answering the question "what if?"

Problems posed to the class for brainstorming may include: What would an ideal writing instrument do? How do you propel an amphibious vehicle? Why is engineering an import subject to study?

Time permitting, the class may engage in a follow-up exercise which encourages more sophisticated consideration of the ideas generated. Each group is asked to classify similar ideas, identifying patterns. After this stage, another brainstorming cycle may be useful to further develop the emerging themes.

Non-Verbal Brainstorming: Why Brainwrite?

- Sometimes called "brainwriting" instead of brainstorming
- Useful with controversial, emotionally charged topics because it is done non-verbally
- Encourages building and developing upon ideas rather than creating further new options

---

Instructors may observe lower participation rates during brainstorming for underrepresented groups, such as non-native English speakers. In this case, brainwriting is a valuable option for increasing participation of students who are reluctant to engage in classroom dialogue. Brainwriting is a non-verbal exercise. It provides a framework that requires all individual team members to express themselves non-verbally. Likewise, it promotes easy synthesis of ideas, by creating a medium which documents the progression of solutions.

Brainwriting: Review the procedure for brainwriting. This activity may be performed with one or more pieces of paper, which contain the same or different topics. Unlike brainstorming, each participant has the "stage" when a recording sheet is placed in their hands, guaranteeing expression of their idea. Brainwriting may take longer than brainstorming, but offers increased participation from each team member. The brainwriting follow-up is identical to brainstorming and asks students to group similar ideas and look for patterns.

Brainwriting: Procedure

Pass around sheet of paper with topic to be addressed written at the top. First person WRITES an idea and each other team member builds on, or adds, to ideas noted

- Done silently
- Cycle paper 3-4 times around group or until people run out of ideas

---

Encourage students to use brainstorming techniques…and reinforce that generating ideas is different from decision making (which has its own set of facilitation tools).

Wrap-Up: Class session wrap-up will depend on the class size, content, and classroom culture. See "Class Adaptation Strategies" at the end of this MIP.

Delivery Plan Part II: Designed for a 90-minute class period

Lecture on Kolb learning style types and team dynamics

This section encourages students to link the information presented in the Interpersonal module to the material covered in the Personal module, specifically Kolb Learning Styles and how these preferences influence team dynamics.

Instructor lecture: Review of Kolb

The instructor reviews the basic Kolb learning styles (see Introductory Personal Knowledge Module for background materials). During this review, students are asked to remember their own learning style preference, and note their group's composition. Considering these differences will highlight much-needed abilities that are often overlooked within project teams, particularly the non-technical skills necessary for project completion. Likewise, remembering individual preference encourages greater tolerance among teammates by asking students to put aside traditional stereotypes.

Review of Kolb Learning Styles

What is a Learning Style?
- Key dimensions
  - Preference for processing or sensing the information
  - Preference for using or judging the information
- Combining dimensions results in 4 types:
  - Divergers (high CE and RO)
  - Assimilators (high RO and AC)
  - Convergers (high AC and AE)
  - Accommodators (high AE and CE)

Style Strengths

Accommodators	Divergers
Getting things done	Being imaginative
Leading	Understanding people
Taking risks	Recognizing problems
Initiating	Brainstorming
Inductive reasoning	Being open-minded
Being adaptable and practical	
IF?	**Why?**
Convergers	**How?** **What?** Assimilators
Solving problems	Planning
Making decisions	Creating models
Defining problems	Defining problems
Being logical	Developing theories
Combining deductive and inductive reasoning	Being patient
	Deductive reasoning

The accompanying slide serves as a reminder of the strengths exhibited by team members with diverse learning style preferences. The slide also includes the signature question for each quadrant. For example, Convergers like to ask the question "How will we get the task accomplished?"

Each learning style contributes something different to a group, yet all components are vital to effective group functioning. At this point, the instructor could note qualities that might be missing if a team lacks members in all learning style categories.

Activity: Predicting behavior based on learning style

Interpersonal effectiveness requires appreciation of different points of view. To this end, the instructor can task the teams to develop a list of how people with each learning style would prefer to accomplish a particular task. An interesting question, also used in the personal knowledge module, asks students to reflect how people with each learning style would prefer to form teams. The following example provides the answers students might provide to this prompt. Discuss the differences between the styles.

Expected Behavior in Teams
(Typical Answers)

	Accommodating	Diverging
Advising Instructor on Team Formation Methods	Prefer informal method	Consider demographics
	Let each member choose	Include student perspective
	Ask professor to discuss team roles first	Develop a process that is optimized for the individual
	Converging	**Assimilating**
	Collect data on skills needed	Set criteria for creating balanced teams
	Collect data on skill sets of students	Balance by GPA's of members
	Create the best teams (make it an equation)	Collect info on students
		Optimize process for task

In engineering, the likelihood of a team being comprised of members representing all four learning styles is small, which may result in the under-representation of certain skills. Therefore, it is extremely important that students learn to compensate for the types of process skills that might be lacking in team interactions.

Remaining aware of different learning style preferences among team members will allow project group members to better understand each other and decrease conflict level. In turn, this knowledge allows team members to manage conflict more maturely should it arise.

Activity: Writing technical instructions

This exercise allows students to use the material previously covered and will appeal to Convergers, who are driven to understand "how" something works.

Exercise: Using Kolb to Enhance Team Skills

- Students divide into groups of diverse learning styles and discuss individual Kolb types
- Brainstorm within group: How do you prefer learning something new (e.g., programming a palm pilot)?
- Groups: Using the results of the brainstorming, write a "how to" set of directions so all learning preferences can get help with the task

Break students into groups, ideally with one member from each LSI preference. Give them the task of designing a set of instructions for how to program a palm pilot or DVD recorder. You might ask different groups to write instructions for different technical objects. The instructions should be effective for all four learning styles.

If a group lacks members with all four learning styles, ask them to use their theoretical knowledge, as presented in the module earlier, and base their instructions for the missing types on that information.

Have the groups share their "instruction guides" with the complete class. The best sets of instructions will include aspects that appeal to each learning style. This activity points out the benefits of having diverse perspectives among team members. First, the process by which the team functions will include the strengths of all four learning styles. Second, the product of the group will have a broader appeal.

 Understanding learning styles differences theoretically and then actually adapting your behavior or the product for use by those with different styles are two separate skills. Knowing both the theory and application is important to successful engineering teamwork.

Activity: Brainstorming about team strengths

This is an activity that allows students to combine what they have learned about brainstorming with their knowledge of learning styles. It works best if students are in their actual project teams.

Have students group themselves according to team assignments and complete the brainstorming exercise using verbal or written brainstorming techniques. Questions should include:

1. Brainstorm the strengths of your team: anything goes!
2. Consider your learning style mix: What are your team's strengths? Weaknesses?
3. Brainstorm ways of getting the missing talents/skills for your team.

Suggestion: Have half the group use verbal brainstorming and the other half brainwriting. Allow time to debrief each method and allow students to consider the different outcomes from the two techniques.

Summary and Wrap-Up. Class session wrap-up will depend on class size, content, and classroom culture. See "Class Adaptation Strategies" at the end of this MIP.

Teaching to the Learning Styles: Interpersonal Effectiveness

CONVERGERS

Brainstorming: These activities are both appealing and challenging to Convergers. Convergers will be happy with a short version of brainstorming because it allows them to develop and present different plausible solutions to the problem. However, they will also want to focus on an early solution and improve it, while resisting expanded brainstorming processes.

Group discussion: Convergers appreciate group discussions that integrate theory and practice. Because they often strain against the confines of lectures, giving them the opportunity to actively solve problems will appeal to their preferences.

Predicting behavior activity: This exercise allows Convergers to answer their favorite question: "how?" Convergers will be comfortable thinking strategically about how individuals with specific learning styles will be expected to behave in teams.

Writing technical instructions: This activity allows Convergers to use their newly learned skills, and provides hands-on experience.

DIVERGERS

Higher level questions: This activity appeals to Divergers, who prefer to know the reasons for doing something as well as how the activity can be beneficial to the members of the team.

Sharing personal experience: When the instructor shares a personal experience that demonstrates the value of good interpersonal skills, this appeals to the Divergers sense of the long-term benefits to individuals as well as their discomfort with insensitive teachers.

Brainstorming team strengths: This activity appeals to Divergers, since they often seek alternate ways to do things. Divergers may engage in a brainstorming activity longer than necessary, as they attempt to ensure that everyone's ideas are shared.

ASSIMILATORS

Introducing learning objectives: When the instructor outlines the merits of interpersonal skills in the team environment, Assimilators become clear about the long term value of their learning.

Formal lecture: This activity satisfies the Assimilator's interest in understanding the general principals for how something works. The lecture provides the key elements necessary for team operation, without necessarily giving the details, which the assimilator may find uninteresting.

ACCOMMODATORS

Brainstorming and brainwriting: This activity is helpful for Accommodator since it provides the tools to have the team work together and develop solutions.

Practicing team communication skills: Accommodators like to integrate experience and application. Subsequently, any activity which allows them to practice new skills and adapt to new situations will appeal to them.

Writing technical instructions: This activity appeals to the Accommodator's wish to move forward with the task at hand. Accommodators traditionally dislike teacher-oriented classrooms, so activities which allow the students to actively participate with the learning will be appreciated.

Class Adaptation Strategies

A. *Size:* In large classes, have students turn to their neighbors (two behind/two in front) to create small groups for brainstorming exercises. The instructor may also facilitate role playing exercises in front of large class (using student volunteers) for giving and receiving feedback scenario, using the teaching assistant as observer.

B. *Content:* In a specific project course, attempt to link brainstorming and feedback exercises to aspects of the project or consider adding student preferences for giving and receiving feedback into team operating procedures or charters. This latter application can facilitate discussion of how team members prefer to receive feedback, and encourages them to consider appropriate ways to provide feedback and the role of feedback in peer evaluation.

C. *Classroom Culture:* Depending on the culture, the instructor might want to identify common assumptions or behaviors that influence the performance of teams. For example, what is the culture's perspective on peers evaluating peers? The instructor may need to explain why giving and receiving feedback from peers is an essential skill to learn even if it difficult. Similarly, the role of the instructor (distant authority, coach, learning facilitator, etc.) might be discussed and student assumptions challenged.

Follow-up Materials

A. Homework: Reading assignment. Instructor choice (see instructor readings and references)

B. Homework: Reflective writing assignment or journal entry. "Are there cultural differences in the ways in which people function in groups that impact listening as well as giving and receiving feedback?" Please explain.

C. Classroom Follow-up: At beginning of next class, ask for volunteers to read their journal entries aloud. If posted electronically to the instructor, have the instructor read anonymous entries and discuss with the class.

D. Exam or Quiz Item: Add questions such as the following to course quizzes or tests. "Describe the strengths and weakness of a selected brainstorming strategy" or "Under what conditions is feedback most likely to be effective?"

4.6 Interpersonal Effectiveness for Students: References

Brassard, M., & Ritter, D. (1994). *The memory jogger II.* Methuen, MA: GOAL/QPC Publishers.

Cook, L., Kling, M., Moy, A., Praske, K., Selenow, T., & Kinney, A. (2000*). Capturing the QUEST mentor experience: A guide to managing student teams.* Unpublished manuscript.

Dally, J. (2001). *Introduction to engineering design: Book 6 (projects and success skills).* Knoxville, TN: College House Enterprises, LLC.

Harb, J.N., & Terry, R.E. (1995). *Writing through the cycle: Application of learning style theory to engineering education at Brigham Young University.* Unpublished manuscript.

Myers, S. (1996). *Team building for diverse work groups.* Irvine, CA: Richard Chang Publications.

Scholtes,P. (1998). *The team handbook.* Madison, WI: Joiner Associates.

Smith, K. (2000). *Project management and teamwork.* Boston: McGraw- Hill.

Chapter 5 BESTEAMS MODULE PROJECT MANAGEMENT

5.1 Introduction to Module

This Module Implementation Plan (MIP) encourages students to use the skills they have learned in earlier modules, including a knowledge of personal preferences and effective interpersonal communication, to help develop methods for project completion. This module is based on the premise that project completion within the engineering context is considerably more complex than other disciplines with which students are familiar. One of BESTEAMS unique attributes is the inclusion of project management training at the undergraduate level. An important component of ensuring timely project completion involves teaching students tools and techniques that will enable them to remain organized and maintain momentum on the project while managing multi-layered tasks.

This module is important because some students, particularly younger individuals, may argue that this type of management is unnecessary. In fact, students (and professionals!) often have difficulty with the longevity of engineering team tasks. Studies have shown that as many as 70% of projects undertaken in the "real world" are not finished within the scheduled deadline (Smith, 2000). Of course, students have the advantage of course terms—generally, a project must be completed within the weeks allotted for the class. However, once students have entered professional positions, they will be held accountable for their project commitments. Learning how to "see the forest for the trees" is vital to ensuring innovative, thorough, and timely project completion. Indeed, appreciation for project management and its associated skills usually grows as students proceed through the engineering curriculum.

Included in this module is a lesson on time management. Underneath every deadline exists an assumption that team members share a common understanding of time as well as the amount of time required to complete the various project components. Even a brief discussion will demonstrate that this is often not the case. Providing students with a common understanding of time and its management is one more necessary tool for ensuring project completion.

5.2 Theoretical Foundations

The practice of project management has existed in some form since humans decided to undertake complex tasks. Conceptually though, project management is essentially a twentieth century endeavor. At its core, "project management is the application of knowledge, tools, and techniques to project activities to meet project requirements" (Project Management Institute, 2000, p. 6). Much of today's project team management literature rests within the business sector; only in recent years have other fields, specifically engineering, chosen to include it within their coursework. While many engineering schools are working to incorporate project management into their curricula, efforts across institutions are uneven. However, for those students who enter industry after finishing their undergraduate work, project management skills are vitally important for their success.

Phases of project management

Project Management experts take different approaches when dividing a large task into actionable pieces. For the purposes of this project, BESTEAMS combines aspects of Weiss and Wysocki's (1992) methodology with the research of Gido and Clements (1999), and breaks Project Management into separate phases: defining the scope of the project, planning the project, implementing and controlling the project, and closing the project. Some authors consider implementing and controlling the project as two separate phases.

Understanding why and how we manage projects are important steps in successfully using the information presented in this module. Often, projects may seem overwhelming when we are faced with all of the complex tasks in their entirety. By segmenting the project into manageable assignments, the multiple priorities facing students will seem less daunting.

Work Breakdown Structure

A work breakdown structure (WBS) is a tool used to subdivide a project into manageable components. The Project Management Institute (2000) defines a WBS as a "deliverable-oriented grouping of project components that organizes and defines the total scope of the project; work not in the WBS is outside the scope of the project" (p. 60). A WBS is comprised of multiple levels that encourage students to identify all of the components of a task. At the lowest level, often called work packages, there are actionable tasks. By breaking a complex project down to smaller pieces, students are able to assign tasks to specific team members and manage the project more effectively.

BESTEAMS agrees that the scoping phase, where students determine the boundaries of the project and its areas of impact, is an integral component to project management and the WBS. However, experience has shown us that novice engineering students generally do not have the project experience needed to adequately understand a lesson on scoping a project. Subsequently, BESTEAMS addresses project scoping in the Intermediate Project Management module. For more information on this module, see **http://www.enme.umd.edu/labs/BESTEAMS/**

Duration

An important characteristic of a project is that individuals work together for a specific time period. Projects have a discrete beginning, middle, and end. On the surface, this may seem overly simplistic. However, when we remember that nearly half of all projects are never finished, the importance of having skills to bring a project to completion becomes clear (Smith, 2000). Hill, Thomas, and Allen (2000) argue that project management effectiveness is a function of how accurate the time estimate is for each task. Essentially, establishing time durations involves estimating the amount of time required to complete each task and subtask of the project. Duration estimates are a necessary prerequisite for creating a *Gantt chart*—a tool which enables students to visualize their project schedule.

There are a number of tools available for determining task durations. The Project Management Institute (2000) identifies four approaches. The first, *expert judgment*, involves taking advantage of people with previous experience regarding the particular task. This may be an individual or a group of people who have specialized knowledge or experience related to the project. "Experts" in this context may be other students, professors, or even outside contacts students may possess. The second approach for determining duration is *analogous estimating*, which uses the actual duration estimate from a previous activity that was similar. *Quantitatively based durations*, the third technique, utilize a formulaic approach which takes advantage of the quantities to be performed for each work category multiplied by the productivity unit rate. For example, if the number of sketches required to design a bridge is four, and it takes two hours to draw each sketch, the total duration for that task will be eight hours. The fourth technique is *reserve time (or contingency)*. In this case, teams add a buffer to their overall completion time, which may be used in the event of unforeseen variations in the project time table. The reserve time is eliminated when it is no longer needed. BESTEAMS offers words of caution regarding the fourth technique. Though it is a safe option thanks to the flexibility it allows, reserving extra, unnecessary time for a project may inflate the project completion time, as project teams spend more time on tasks than actually necessary. For these reasons, the fourth technique should not be overly encouraged, especially for novice project management students.

This working backwards approach to time duration, while sometimes laborious, is essential to accurately estimating the number of hours required to complete a project. By looking at the durations that individual tasks will require, students can roughly estimate the number of hours an entire project will consume. Important to remember, however, is that the total time a project will take cannot be finalized until the project teams identify how the activities link together (known as dependences). Often after identifying dependencies, the team members will need to review their time durations to ensure the project will be completed by the instructor's deadline.

Dependencies

Dependencies are relationships between activities or tasks. In some cases, a number of subtasks must be completed in a specific sequence before beginning the next step of a project. Other times, subtasks are independent from each other, and project completion does not require a specific ordering of the tasks. Also called logical relationships, there are four possible types of dependencies that exist between tasks. *Finish-to-start dependencies* are those in which one activity must be finished before another may begin. For example, a part must be designed before it can be built. *Finish-to-finish* dependencies are those in which one activity must finish before another can finish, and are most commonly used in project management. To illustrate, a professor cannot submit her grades to the registrar until she evaluates the final assignments. *Start-to-start* activities are those in which the initiation of a task depends upon the initiation of a previous task. For instance, some members of the team cannot begin writing the project until they receive some of the results from their teammates. *Start-to-finish* dependencies are those in which one task may not be completed until a previous task is started. This particular dependency is rarely used, and then only by professional scheduling managers (Project Management Institute, 2000).

Gantt chart

The developer of the Gantt chart, Henry Gantt (1861-1915), studied the order of operations of projects in the early twentieth century. Sisk (n.d.) reports, "His Gantt charts, complete with task bars and milestone markers, outline the sequence and durations of all tasks in a process" (p. 1). Although other tools have been developed to outline project components, the Gantt chart remains a preferred instrument for introductory-level project management instruction, due in part to the straightforward design.

The Gantt chart is a graphical representation of the WBS that displays activity start and end dates, expected durations, and dependencies. Likewise, resources and accountability for various tasks can be shown directly next to each activity. For nearly one hundred years, Gantt's original design remained unchanged from the technique just described. Then in the early 1990s, link lines were added to task bars in order to depict more precise dependencies between tasks (Sisk, n.d.). In the revised Gantt chart, time increments are on the X axis and the activities are on the Y axis. Different markers and symbols depict the relationships that exist between tasks.

Many software packages, such as Microsoft® Project and ProjectInsight®, have been developed to facilitate Gantt chart creation. These products generally ask the project manager to input data about milestones, tasks, durations, and dependencies and then produce a Gantt chart for the user. Software packages are particularly useful because changes can be easily made to certain components, such as the durations or dependencies, and the Gantt chart will be adjusted accordingly.

Time Management

The concept of time is paradoxical. On one hand, nothing is more obvious than the common notion of time as a limited resource. On the other hand, it is a largely unexamined universally accepted concept. Time becomes particularly pressing for first-year undergraduates, when inexperience may result in a perceived inability to complete new college responsibilities. Students are often faced with a sense of fixed time in which seconds tick away and days pass beyond their control. They may develop coping mechanisms that rarely contain any real mastery over time, yet represent the sole plan for finishing tasks. Poor time management often manifests itself in procrastinating behaviors. However, many students would say that the one thing they want to overcome is procrastination. Exposing students to a new perspective of time may help them overcome this obstacle.

Our concept of time is both historic, instinctive, and informed by those around us and *their* understanding of time (Szamosi, 1986). The belief that time is fixed allows for little control, so attempts to manage time may be viewed as fruitless endeavors by students. Instead, a new perspective on the nature of time is needed that will empower students to accomplish tasks. The goal is to have students focus on what they want to accomplish within a specific time frame, rather than learn how to manage time itself. This paradigm shift is accomplished by focusing on commitments in time. Students are asked to think about personal time management in much the same way as they would a Gantt chart: what activities must be started and completed within a particular time frame?

To help students view the nature of time more complexly, begin by examining the history of calendars. Culkin (1986) chronicles the attempts made by various cultural groups to address the difficulty of fitting days, hours, and minutes into either a solar or lunar calendar, and illustrates how altering the calendar negatively impacted society. For example, in the sixteenth century Pope Gregory XIII removed eleven days from the calendar in order to align it with the seasons and people revolted—they thought they had lost those days from their lives! People existing within a paradigm come to view that structure as reality (Culkin, 1986). National holidays provide another example around which individuals from different cultures structure their concepts of time. For those living in the United States, Thanksgiving or Independence Day may define important aspects of our lives. In contrast, these dates do not have meaning or memories for those outside of the U.S.

Other theorists have considered the ways in which humans view time. In his article "The Origins of Time," Szamosi (1986) examines the evolution of the definition and quantification of time, arguing that the need to quantify and measure time is solely a human phenomenon. Starting in the prehistoric age, the segmentation of temporal occurrences moved with biological demands: the days were determined by the sun's motion and the months were marked by the moon. As tribes expanded into societies, seasons where planting or harvesting occurred were gradually designated by holidays. At that point in history, there were no concepts of hours, minutes or seconds. The unit of day was specific enough for most of life's activities. Compare that view with the certainty modern humanity holds that seconds, minutes, and hours both exist and are essential.

The concept of fixed time as we know it today evolved from the Gregorian monks' concept of polyophony, the singing of complex melodies and note durations (Szamosi, 1986). To create a musical composition, the composer needed to generate the construct of fixed intervals to coordinate the integrated actions of many voices. In those centuries, the scientific and religious heads were also the philosophers who contributed to the cultural practices. Thus, the concept of fixed intervals of "time" began to enter into the human experience as a tool to coordinate activities. The Gregorian chant became a time construct and was the basis upon which Galileo and later Newton posited that time was a dimension separate from space and objects (Szamosi, 1986).

The notion that time could be useful as a measurement tool evolved from the experiments of Galileo. Galileo was the first in Western culture to argue that time was an independent variable. Indeed, if we accept that time is a construct, then we may reasonably argue that he was the first person to actually time an event, during his seventeenth century experiment in which he dropped two cannonballs from the Leaning Tower of Pisa. According to Galileo's research, time existed in relation to the changing location of physical objects. Newton (1687) later codified the view: "Absolute, true, and mathematical time, of itself, and from its own nature flows equably without regard to anything external, and by another name is called duration: relative, apparent, and common time, is some sensible and external (whether accurate or unequable) measure of duration by the means of motion, which is commonly used instead of true time; such as an hour, a day, a month, a year" (*The Principia*, p. 4).

The development of time measuring devices has also evolved. Initially there was a need for accurate measurement of length and volume but there was little need for, or appreciation of, the measurement of time (Szamosi, 1986). Calendars were used by people to organize societies over long periods. The creation of an apparatus to measure time grew out of the development of devices designed to document the motion of the planets and the occurrence of other natural phenomena. Only when fixed increments of time were conceived and mechanical capabilities improved were clocks created. As societies became more complex, increasingly accurate distinctions of time were required. The advent of the industrial age, where numerous individuals performed integrated tasks, resulted in the creation of time clocks. As the global economy grew, more complex clocks allowed for the coordination of even more complicated activities. Indeed, the establishment of Greenwich Mean Time provided the point from which all other times are measured around the world. Today, computers have created the parsing of time down to the nanosecond to coordinate the global internet. At this level of differentiation, the quantification of time is far removed from the biological distinctions necessary for human experience.

To fully appreciate the development of time through history, Heidegger's (1956) view regarding time's relationship with human existence must be considered. Heidegger observed that there is no measurement of time without man. The two—the occurrence of time and the expression of the individual—are intimately related. An example illustrates this insight: when first learning to play tennis, an individual's response to a fast serve is likely minimal. However, after developing some skill in the game, though the same type serve comes across the net, the individual now has a variety of optional responses, such as choosing to hit a cross-court return or slamming the ball down the line. In the domain of clock time, the actual seconds it takes for the ball to come across the net is exactly the same for the novice and experienced player. However, the person's response is perceived to be vastly different. The experienced player senses more options whereas the novice is flummoxed by the fast flying serve. What is different between the two players is not the management of time itself, but the *experience* of that time. In other sports, the same phenomenon is reported by knowledgeable players. In baseball, batters talk about the pitched ball looking as large as a grapefruit. In basketball, shooters talk about the basket looking as big as a crate. Thus, time and individual perception are intimately correlated.

Moving from a biological temporal sense to an arbitrarily set yet rigidly maintained sense of fixed time has created a reality in which people find themselves trying to manage something that controls them rather than anything they have authority over. As a result of living within a fixed sense of time, many people feel rushed, experience an inability to enjoy and complete activities, and are run by to-do lists that do not take into account what may actually be accomplished. Watts (1975) explains, "The idea of separate events, which have to be linked by a mysterious process called cause and effect, is

5.4 50-Minute Class Overview: Introductory Project Management

---

Module Outline
- Introduce objectives of lesson
- Ask broad questions to generate discussion about project management
- Deliver formal lecture on the stages of project management
- Explain work breakdown structures
- Facilitate group work on project resources/time durations/dependencies
- Introduce the Gantt chart

Expected student outcomes
- Insight into the need for long term planning
- Insight into the uses of a Work Breakdown Structure and Gantt charts, and practice using them
- Insight and greater ease when placing activities within time and distributing specific responsibilities

Assessment/Homework Options
- Add questions in midterm or final exam
- Assign teamwork reading assignment: instructor choice
- Assign reflective writing assignment

Materials Needed
- PowerPoint Slides
- Computer
- Projector
- Large sheets of paper for groups
- Markers to use for writing on paper

90-Minute Class Overview: Extended Class Outline & Additional Outcomes

---

Extended Class Outline
- Discuss the ways in which students facilitate their own time management
- Establish the historic background of time
- Create awareness of commitments and their connection to time management

Additional Expected Outcomes
- Insight into the role time management plays in project completion
- Insight into the way time affects the project completion cycle
- Insight into the notion of managing commitments
- Insight into the importance of scheduling

5.5 BESTEAMS Module Implementation Plan (MIP)
Introductory Level Project Management

Topic: *Project Management for First-Year Students*

Tracks	Personal Knowledge	Interpersonal Effectiveness	Project Management
Introductory	Kolb Learning Styles	Team Development & Communications Basics	Managing Your Project: Planning & Time

Introduction/Motivation

Managing Your Project: Planning & Time

Introductory Project Management Module

This MIP addresses several key aspects of *project management* within student project teams. The fundamental planning tools presented in this module include 1) Work Breakdown Structures (WBS) for identifying the necessary actions in sufficient detail so students can effectively act, and 2) Gantt charts which place the activities in time and identify dependencies between the activities. Subsequent modules introduce the topics of scoping a project, tracking a project over the semester, dealing with breakdowns in a project, and closing out a project.

The complete PowerPoint® presentation shown in this module, as well as subsequent material, is available for download at
http://www.enme.umd.edu/labs/BESTEAMS/

Expected Outcomes

As a result of implementing this module, students should experience positive outcomes that will facilitate the development of useful team project skills, including.

Module Part I

- Insight into the need for long term planning
- Insight into creating and using Work Breakdown Structures and Gantt charts
- Insight and greater ease when placing activities within a time frame and distributing specific responsibilities among team members

Project Management Learning Objectives

- Establish an understanding of basic project planning and scheduling skills
- Learn how to use several basic tools
  - Work breakdown structures
  - Resource allocation
  - Gantt charts

Module Part II

- Insight into the role time management plays in project completion
- Insight into the ways time affects the project completion cycle
- Insight into the notion of managing commitments
- Insight into the importance of scheduling

Delivery Plan Part I: Designed for a 50-minute class period

Introduce the module and its objectives. Class characteristics should be considered when determining the best method for presenting the expected outcomes—in other words, is your class filled with first-year students who might be intimidated by the material? Is your class comprised of upper-level students, who will think they understand the concepts with relative ease? The speed with which the material is presented may change according to these answers. Along with stating the objectives, the instructor's goal is to establish the student's interest in the topic and this module by encouraging a personal investment in the subject. When introducing the material, one

---

Appreciating Project Management

- Studies report that as many as 70% of all projects initiated are not completed
- Engineering projects are multifaceted– they consist of complex interdependent tasks

---

way to engage the class is to ask about their experience with projects, project management, and time lines or other scheduling tools.

Introduction to Project Management terminology

Questions to initiate discussions include: What is a project? What are its components? After discussing the responses to these questions, show students the definition. It should be emphasized that projects are complex and involve many interrelated tasks for completion. In addition, projects can only be completed through effective resource use (for example, people and equipment). It may be useful to differentiate a project from a simple to- do list. While a to-do list contains a series of activities that must be accomplished, it lacks the project components outlined on the accompanying slide, including: an overarching single objective that connects the activities, interrelatedness of the activities, and specific schedules for completion.

What is a Project?

- A project has a single objective that must be accomplished through the completion of tasks that are unique and interrelated
- Projects are completed through the deployment of resources
- Projects have scopes, schedules, and costs and are accomplished within specific deadlines, budgets, and according to specification

---

 Introducing students to the value of the module is a first step in creating a successful learning environment.

Establish class participation by helping students recall projects that did not go well for them. An example might be a time when they stayed up late to complete an assignment, and were still unable to finish it. This helps to engage the students' interest by drawing direct real world connections to the topic. At this point, the instructor may also ask the class members about their experiences in projects and project management, including the use of timelines and other methods for organizing activities. This section will appeal to Divergers, who learn by asking the question: "Why?" Remind the students that no matter what the planning, once the project actually begins, everything starts to shift and go out of balance. Identify the aspects that could occur that would alter the equilibrium. For example, information may be harder to find than imagined or the original concept as stated may turn out to be too large in scope.

In the beginning, we know we can manage our projects but before long...

Time   Money

Activity: Project planning

Ask students to identify a project for use during the module. This activity is helpful when students have a class project on which to focus. The project planning process is much more complex than creating a to-do list. To clarify the distinction, have students identify, articulate, and agree upon the main goal. Ask some of the students to share the project they will use during the lesson. The instructor should take into account individual student characteristics, including language abilities, gender, and level of experience with team projects.

Project Planning Activity

Identify a class project to use during this lesson

- What is your project's name?
- What is the main goal of your team's project?

Instructor Lecture

Project Management Stages: Review the stages of project management and remind students that this module focuses on **Develop the Plan**. Explain to them that they may receive information on the other phases in subsequent courses they will take. The stage in which students implement the plan and control the process contains mechanisms which provide feedback on how the project progresses in real time. Based on this information, plans may need to be altered according to unforeseen events that occur. Closing the project will require reviewing all project planning phases so the students can learn from their experience.

Phases of Project Management

- Define the project's scope
- Develop the project's plan
- Implement the plan & control the process
- Close out the project

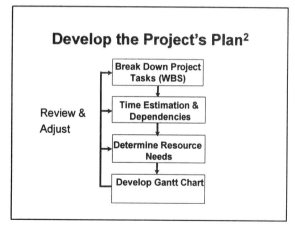

Develop the project's plan: The accompanying slide depicts the four steps used to develop the plan. The final deliverable of this module will be a Gantt chart, which assembles information from the Work Breakdown Structure (WBS), task duration estimates, dependencies, and resource allocations. At each step in the process, changes can be made until the team members have a Gantt chart that they agree will be their plan of action, and that would pass their manager's approval.

Work Breakdown Structure (WBS)

Creating a WBS allows the team to identify the project tasks. This section is designed to foster thought about the activities students need to accomplish for the project. The first step identifies the major project components. Once the main activities have been labeled, they are divided into actionable pieces. Students should also identify major milestones—significant project accomplishments—such as completion of project design, interim reports, and the final product. Once this material has been covered, students should understand that projects have multiple, interrelated tasks. Walking students through a variety of examples is especially helpful.

Define the WBS: When discussing Work Breakdown Structures, it is helpful to develop familiar analogies for the students. This slide's main message is that dividing the project into activities in a logical manner creates a landscape of coordinated team actions which can be viewed and managed. Without the WBS's hierarchical structure, the information provided would just be another to-do list.

What is a Work Breakdown Structure (WBS)?

- It is a hierarchical representation of activities
- It starts with the major project areas to be accomplished
- It breaks the project areas into actionable pieces of work, segmenting elements into appropriate sublevels

WBS – Activity Levels

- Level 1 – Identify major objective areas or categories
- Level 2 – Begin to divide the areas into sub-tasks
- Level 3 – Continue to break down the sub-tasks into actionable items
- The lowest level associated with a branch in the hierarchy is referred to as a "work package"

    # of levels depends on project complexity

Discuss the levels of the WBS: Within each project component, the WBS is a hierarchical ordering from the objective level to that of specific actionable items. A sufficient number of levels must be identified to allow for implementation and monitoring without overwhelming the project with minutia. The appropriate number of levels has been achieved when an outsider may look at the WBS and understand how the project will be fulfilled. As a warning: Students may be tempted to map the syllabus onto a timeline without identifying the tasks necessary to fulfill the deliverables. Instructors should monitor this tendency.

When a project is broken down into actionable pieces, it is easier to estimate the time and cost of each activity

When creating a WBS, the first task is to identify the major components of the project. Using an example will help the students understand the process in creating a WBS. The accompanying slide offers an example from the Introduction to Engineering Design class at the University of Maryland, College Park (Fourney, 2002). When introduced to this notion, students were asked: "What are the functions involved with designing a crane?" An important idea to mention regarding this activity is that different individuals will offer varying level 1 activities, depending on the way they conceptualize the project. This activity encourages students to identify as many high level activities as possible (Level 1). At this level, there is no detail on how to accomplish any of the tasks.

**WBS: Crane Example
Level 1 Activities**

1. Design support columns
2. Analyze fasteners
3. Design trolley hoist
4. Design beams and crane span
5. Produce final report

Proceeding with the crane example will illustrate how the different levels are segmented. Essentially, a WBS serves as a microscope with different levels of magnification that reveal increasing detail. When working through these ideas, the instructor may select one of the high level activities and demonstrate how to sub-divide the activity into smaller tasks. The subdivision should continue until the resulting pieces are actionable, measurable tasks. The accompanying slide provides an example for the support column.

WBS: Crane Example (cont'd)

1. Design support columns (Level 1)
   1.1 Select final material (Level 2)
      1.1.1 Design for compression (Level 3)
      1.1.2 Design for buckling (Level 3)
      1.1.3 Calculate deformation (Level 3)

Activity: Identifying sub-tasks

After working through this example, select another high level activity and have the students attempt to identify the sub-tasks on their own. Once this has been completed, lead a class discussion about the students' choices and level of detail.

WBS: Crane Example (cont'd)

6. Produce final report
   6.1 Write text
   6.2 Produce drawings
   6.3 Exhibit sample calculations

Continuation of instructor lecture

This final slide on the crane example addresses project components that students may consider ancillary to the task at hand, such as writing the report. This concept of completeness—including every task on the WBS—is important. Students must understand that all aspects of the project should be accounted for in their WBS, including the creating of the reports, completing related homework assignments, and developing presentations.

Discussion: Determining WBS detail

At this time, the instructor facilitates a discussion about the amount of detail required to develop a thorough WBS. The accompanying slide contains some prompts that will help students determine when they have a complete WBS. Learning the appropriate balance for amount of detail in the WBS is important—too little nearly guarantees overlooking important aspects while too much will eclipse the primary goals. Though this skill can be difficult for students at first, mastering this ability is essential in organizing successful projects.

> ## How much detail do you need?[1,2]
>
> - Does the WBS contain enough detail to evaluate progress?
>   - Do you have clear accountability for each work package?
>   - Are there start & end events?
>   - Can you easily estimate time & cost?
>   - Is there a clearly defined deliverable?

 Developing the WBS is an iterative process; it may take several tries to identify all tasks in the appropriate level of detail.

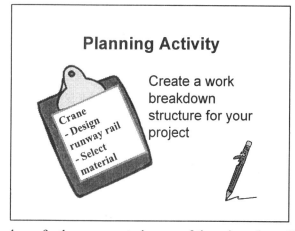

Planning Activity

Create a work breakdown structure for your project

Crane
- Design runway rail
- Select material

Activity: Developing a WBS in teams

Distribute students into their project teams so they can begin creating a WBS for their team's project. Students should be prompted to work on one or two of the main components, designating a sufficient number of levels. The actionable task should be the last level identified. The instructor can interrupt the teams midway through the activity to ensure progress by discussing any questions from students. After this break, teams should return to the task, ensuring that they have identified all of the Level 1 activities for their project and have further segmented some of them into the sufficient number of sub-levels.

Discussion: Time duration

The next discussion in this module is time. Helping students understand the concepts of time duration, estimation, and variation will provide them with valuable tools when working to achieve project completion. There is a larger context in which the project fits. Encouraging students to recognize how their project activities fit within the context of their other obligations (such as classes, work schedules, and family) will help them develop more realistic expectations for their project.

Each task within a project will require a certain amount of effort and time to complete. Effort refers to the number of hours a specific task will require for completion, while time identifies the span over which the activity will occur. For example, getting a cost-quote from a company may take two weeks of time but will require very little effort on the part of the team member assigned that task. Understanding the relationship between these two is necessary when making personnel resource allotments.

Time Duration

Managing a project requires awareness of two time frames

1. The amount of effort a task will take (in time), e.g., 3 hours to write a report

2. The calendar span over which the activity will occur, e.g., the report will be done within a week

---

Time Estimation

* If feasible, have person responsible make the estimate
* Should take into account the resources needed for the activity
* Do not overestimate to account for everything that can go wrong
* Keep in mind the concept of self-fulfilling prophecy

The first step in identifying time durations requires students to hypothesize how long specific components of their projects will last. Students may initially be resistant to guessing how much time a task might take: It may be necessary to help them identify ways to make educated guesses. Encourage students to ask the person responsible for each task to estimate the amount of time required to complete the task. Help the students understand that time duration may vary based on availability and amount of resources. Discourage them from relying on overestimates that allow for every possible contingency of what can go wrong. Remind them of self-fulfilling prophecies: When you set expectations (low or high) you often perform to that level.

An aim of this module is to encourage students to understand that the best laid plans do not always occur according to schedule. Uncertainty is a given when developing schedules. Variation—unexpected events occurring and false assessments of individual abilities—is a natural part of project implementation. There are numerous causes for variation that must be considered during the creation of the project plan. Similarly, some maturity is required to maintain calm in the face of unplanned situations. Knowing how to handle uncertainty well is important for effective teams.

Uncertainty in Time Estimates

* Some activities will take longer and others will go faster than expected
* Sources of uncertainty:
  * Varying knowledge and skills
  * Individual difference in approaching work
  * Mistakes or misunderstandings
  * *Unexpected events (!!)*

Activity: Estimating durations

For this activity, students turn to their project teams and, using the WBS previously created, estimate the time duration for each task at the lowest level (called work packages). With respect to time duration, students must quantify the time and effort needed for the task as well as the potential variation. It is important to emphasize that variation estimates are not arbitrary. For example, a chemistry lab is only open at certain fixed times. If the team fails to accomplish the task there, the members will have to wait to finish the assignment until the lab is open again.

Project Planning Activity

- For each work package, estimate the time duration in days

Continuation of instructor lecture: Resources

In this section, a discussion of resources encourages students to think beyond the WBS. Resources, both tangible and personal, are an important component of any successful team project. Deliberate consideration about them is required to ensure all resources, both internal (e.g., team members) and external (e.g., experts), are properly utilized.

Identifying Resources[1, 2]

To accomplish each activity identified in the WBS requires the use of resources:

- Personnel (who, how many, their skills)
- Space (meeting location, lab facilities)
- Equipment (rent, own, purchase, how long needed)
- Money (budget limitations)

Discuss the various resources needed to complete the project. Note that time is not included on this resource list. As a part of this section, be sure to include a dialogue on the additional materials and supplies that may not be immediately obvious, for example, paper for printing final reports and presentation equipment. It is important that students identify one person who will be accountable for each specific task. This is true even if more than one person, or the whole team, works on the task; one person is ultimately responsible for execution and completion of the task.

The instructor should help students understand that the way they assign resources to a project can affect their project. The assignment of resources is sometimes referred to as resource loading. A critical aspect of resource loading is to balance effort over time, so that tasks are distributed evenly. A common error is assigning one person or resource to multiple overlapping tasks without taking into account the effort required, which may result in partially completed tasks. The manner in which resources are allocated can impact the speed with which the project is completed and the quality of the outcome.

Assigning Resources

- Assign resources to the appropriate tasks (personnel, space, equipment, money)
- Be realistic– no one can be in two places at one time

Instructors may want to consider their own learning goals for the project prior to a discussion about how to assign resources. For example, if the instructor wants everyone to experience all aspects of the project, resources will need to be assigned differently than if the instructor wants a project that is completed with high efficiency. The tradeoff between these two approaches becomes the broader impact on student learning.

Activity: Identifying personnel resources

Ask the students to identify the personnel resources required for their project. Discuss what students have identified to see if they are completely thinking through their project needs. Depending on the class size, brainstorming or brainwriting (see Introductory Interpersonal Module) may prove useful. Having students share their answers with each other will encourage groups to consider what might be missing on their own lists.

Project Planning Activity

What are the resources needed for each task in the WBS?

Continuation of instructor lecture: Dependencies

Within a project, there are relationships that exist between tasks, called dependencies. There are numerous types, as discussed in the Theoretical Foundations section of this module, but the Finish-to-Start relationship is the easiest to understand. A Finish-to-Start relationship is one where the new task cannot begin until an earlier task has been finished.

By building dependencies between tasks, the structure of the schedule is created. Dependencies tell us when activities can start and when they can end. Ultimately, these dependencies tell team members the minimum time in which the project can be finished based on their time duration estimates. After identifying the dependencies, the resource assignments should be reviewed to ensure team members are not assigned to be in two places at once.

Dependencies

Dependencies are the relationships between activities

"Finish-to-Start" example

Predecessor Task: A

Successor Task: B

Arrow head indicates dependency relationship: Task B cannot begin until Task A is complete

Examples of other dependency types:
-start-to-finish
-start-to-start
-finish-to-finish

Project Planning Activity

- Number all tasks in your WBS
- Identify the dependencies between each task

  Notice at what level you are identifying the dependency. How does the dependency affect higher or lower level activities?

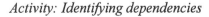

Activity: Identifying dependencies

In their groups, students should define all the dependencies that exist between the tasks identified in their WBS. This can be confusing depending on how well the students understand the individual tasks and the interrelatedness of the activities. For example, if they identify a dependency between level 1 activities it is implied that all of the associated lower level activities are also dependent. The instructor should ensure that students are clear on that concept before moving forward with the module.

Continuation of instructor lecture: Gantt charts

In this section, the instructor introduces the concept of the Gantt chart and its uses. The Gantt chart is a visual scheduling tool that provides an overall summary of the tasks, resources, time estimates, and dependencies. Developing the Gantt chart requires close attention to, and a willingness to revise, the details. After laying out the activities, students may find they have set unrealistic expectations for their project, at which point they will need to go back and make adjustments. If available, using project management software is helpful at this point. Gantt charts constructed with pencil and paper become messy and difficult to read (Smith, 2004).

**The Gantt Chart:
A Visual Scheduling Tool**

- Graphically represents WBS information
- Shows dependencies between tasks, time duration, personnel, and other resource allocations
- Tracks progress towards project completion

Building a Gantt Chart: Axes

- List all tasks and milestones from the WBS along the vertical axis
- List time frame along the horizontal axis

Tasks:
Design support columns
Select final material
Design...

Time Frame: day 1 day 2 day 3

Walk students through the process of creating a Gantt chart. Gantt charts can take on a variety of formats. However, there are two things that all charts will have in common: a list of tasks on one axis and a time frame or calendar on the other axis. Other useful features may include, for each task, the amount of effort required, the time duration, and resource allotment. These elements result in a complete road map for the students and the instructor. In other words, this is a visual display of the way the project will proceed in time. It provides the students with a realistic portrayal of what is required to fulfill the project, as well as the

knowledge that it can be done.

Gantt charts have different symbols to represent different kinds of activities. Various software packages will use different conventions. For example, the convention shown in the accompanying slide is that use by Microsoft® Project. The thick black bars denote higher level activities, which may have many sub-tasks (white bars), milestones (diamonds), or other higher level activities associated with their individual deadlines.

Building a Gantt Chart: Dependencies

Depict dependencies between activities using arrows or lines

For example: Design for compression cannot begin until materials are chosen

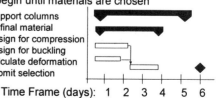

Design support columns
Select final material
Design for compression
Design for buckling
Calculate deformation
Submit selection

Time Frame (days): 1 2 3 4 5 6

Project Planning Activity

Based on the WBS (tasks, durations, and dependencies) create a Gantt Chart

Activity: Creating a Gantt chart

In this activity, students build a Gantt chart for their project. The instructor should circulate through the classroom while students complete this section, answering questions and providing advice. A common error when designing Gantt charts is forgetting to include the dependencies between tasks. At the end of the activity, the instructor should ask the teams what aspects were the most difficult to learn. If class time is running short, students may be asked to complete the Gantt chart as a homework assignment.

Continuation of instructor lecture: Team responsibility

As the lesson nears its conclusion, the instructor must help students move from the planning stage of a project to the action stage. This involves ensuring students take ownership of their own action items as well as remain aware of the other team member tasks that must be completed. At this stage in the lesson, a discussion of the links between accountability and responsibility may help clarify the issue.

Next Step: Implement the Plan

After the plan is complete, everyone should know who is responsible for each activity and when each task must be complete to ensure project success

Responsibility Matrix

• Creates accountability by assigning each task to a person

Task	Joe	Marie	Renee
Activity 1		x	
Activity 2	x		
Activity 3			x

A resource matrix may be a useful tool for building accountability. This is simply a matrix with one team member's name per row with each activity in a single column. An "X" is used to indicate who is responsible for the various activities. An important concept to emphasize is that each person is accountable for his or her specific tasks, but ultimately the group is responsible for the success of the project.

The other issue that comes into play once the team in is action is the unpredictability of personal and team expectations. Students might not like it, but what people said they can do versus what they will do can change. Learning how to correct for these shifts is necessary for meeting project milestones.

Before concluding this module, an important concept worth mentioning is that of billable hours. When students become working professionals, they are held accountable for the time they spend on different components of a project. Although this does not apply to the students yet, encouraging them to think as professionals will help them tie this lesson into their larger goals. This activity will particularly appeal to Divergers, who like to understand the implications of their actions. In addition, if teams experience difficulty with workload equity, keeping a billable hour log may be a useful tool to help diffuse the problem.

Project Planning Summary

- Create WBS to identify activities
- Estimate time durations
- Identify resource needs
- Note dependencies between tasks
- Schedule activities using a Gantt chart
- Review plan until you reach agreement

    Put plan into action!

As the lesson concludes, help students recognize what they have learned by asking: What do the terms "Work Breakdown Structure", "Gantt chart", and "resource allocation" describe? The instructor should describe from his or her own experience what these terms mean, and their importance when conducting a successful project.

Summarize the lesson by reviewing each of the project management steps covered in this module. The instructor can emphasize these points by linking the elements to their team project expectations. The instructor should also consider what he or she would like to assign for homework, in order to ensure that students integrate the lesson's material with their independent learning. Other characteristics to be considered when wrapping up the module include how to link the lesson with classroom culture and content. See Class Adaptation Strategies at the end of this module.

Managing Your Project:
Planning & Time

References

1. Van Aken, S. (2001). *University Leadership Development*. Virginia Tech, Blacksburg, VA.
2. Weiss, J.W., & Wysocki, R.K. (1992). *5-Phase Project Management: A Practical Planning and Implementation Guide*. Reading, MA: Addison Wesley.

Delivery Plan Part II: Designed for a 90-minute class session

Though included as a supplement to the Project Management module, this section may also be offered as a stand-alone lesson.

Managing Your Projects: Time

What does it take to create something bigger than yourself?

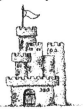

This section addresses key aspects of time management within student project teams. Students will learn fundamental skills for creating and operating a project schedule. For many younger students the instructor must address maintaining a personal time management system as a required precursor to appreciating the requirements for a project management structure. The goal of this module is to move student focus from managing time to managing accomplishments in time. This will be achieved through an assignment where they write down all commitments, schedule them, and then track what they actually do for one week.

Introduce the module and the objectives

An important point of this module unpacks the common perception that projects are supposed to run smoothly. In reality, most team members will have to respond to multiple changes throughout the course of the project. Since a project team is comprised of many individuals, each with his or her own schedule, the fluctuating project schedule necessarily interfaces with these personal schedules. The effective intermeshing of the two is necessary for successful completion of the project and individual satisfaction.

Learning Objectives

- Understand the need for tracking personal time management
- Conceptualize the difference between managing commitments and managing time

Introduction to project management terminology

What Characterizes a Project?

- Consists of orchestrated activities
- Creates and causes something to occur
- Calls people to action

Before showing the accompanying slide, ask students for their definition of a project. If students have just completed the first section of the module (Project Management planning) these slides may be unnecessary. However, this brief overview provides appropriate context for the time management information that follows.

After developing a short list of project components, the instructor can show this slide, which offers a working definition. If students are having difficulty conceptualizing this point, providing an example might be useful. For instance, building a car is a project that requires extensive management. In contrast, controlling the weather is impossible. A key element of a project that students must understand is that they are creating something—a project—that does not exist already, with knowledge and skills that they may or may not have, and team members who represent an unknown situation. Coordinating a project is important, but hard, work.

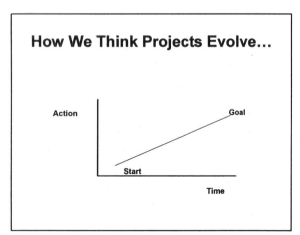

Discussion: Connecting actions and time

Ask students how they think projects should evolve. The accompanying slide depicts the common perception. Important for students to note in this graph is that time and action are the two independent variables on the X and Y axes—their interaction creates the link between the project beginning and its completion. Most students assume a direct, straightforward relationship between beginning the task and completing it. Experienced project managers know that is seldom the case.

In reality, most projects show forward progress as well as some false starts. A better depiction of a typical engineering project looks like the picture on the accompanying slide. As before, time and action are on the x and y axes, and the project's trajectory arises from the interaction of the two. Most projects, even ones that are working, evolve in a similar, nonlinear fashion. Students should be reminded that some backtracking is okay, particularly if it corrects for future problems.

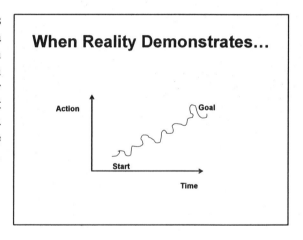

 Every project has unexpected setbacks and windfalls. Project Management ensures that this variation is taken into account in such a way that the project can be completed.

Instructor lecture and discussion: Time management

At this point in the lesson, the material moves to a discussion of time. Understanding how time is perceived in society is important for creating common understanding. Another discussion point is the notion that we did not create time. Rather, we live in time. However, we cannot manage what we did not create—we can only manage what we do within the time we are given.

The accompanying slide provides a list of common methods for tracking time. Students may be asked to brainstorm a list, if the instructor wishes for classroom participation. The questions on the bottom of the slide encourage students to take ownership of the material to be addressed, and consider ways to incorporate the material into their daily processes. These can be answered individually by students or as a question and answer session with the instructor.

Methods to Track Time

- Time management planners or schedulers
- PDAs
- A piece of paper to write things down
- Memory

What problems do you have in the area of time management?

What do you want to get out of this conversation on time management?

History of Time

- How was time measured?
  - Observation of sunrise and sunset
  - Evolved to Solar and Lunar calendars
  - Humans developed mechanical clocks

Look at the evolution of time throughout history. As a preliminary assignment, the students may be given readings on the subject (see sources cited in Theoretical Foundations for this module). The instructor can go through the readings, highlighting important topics. Possible questions include:

- What was the experience of time for prehistoric people? What was the increment of time? Did they have seconds?
- Question: When did fixed time come into existence? Answer: The Gregorian monks wanted to sing together and established fixed time. Factor in the industrial revolution and an expanding need for global coordination and we have ended up with nanoseconds.

Our current experience of time has three characteristics: It's fixed, it's outside of us and our control, and there is never enough of it.

People's sense of time has altered over the centuries. We currently live in a reality of fixed time, resulting in a feeling of scarcity and constant pressure.

Nature of Time

Q: Is time like a sail boat or a motor boat?

A: It's more like a sail boat in a shifting wind
- Tennis Example
- Vacation Example

10

In this section, students should be encouraged to question the notion of fixed time. The instructor should provide examples of the elasticity of time. Once students understand, ask them for examples of their own.

Possible examples include:
1) Learning to play tennis. Suppose you are new player and you are standing across from an expert. When the expert serves, the ball will pass you before you can respond. But after you become more experienced, for the same serve, you may now determine various possible returns. The ball is traveling in the same time but your ability to respond has changed.

2) Your perception of how many tasks may be accomplished before vacation compared to a rainy Monday. Often we find that the more we have to accomplish, the more gets done. What has changed about those days? Though the *fixed* time has remained the same, the *experience* of time often changes when there is much to be done.

At this juncture, students should begin to understand that time itself cannot be controlled. But if you do not manage time, what do you manage?

- Take answers from the students
- Encourage them to consider that commitments are managed, not time
- Introduce discussion topic: When considering time management, the only thing individuals can control is their commitments. Understanding this distinction is an important one for students.

What Do You Manage?

- You do not manage time
- You manage your commitments

The only thing you have power over is whatever you say yes or no to. You have the power to manage your commitments.

Start to clarify the nature of commitments, so that students begin with a common theoretical framework. This section may be offered in lecture format or as a discussion, depending on classroom characteristics. Questions to ask students may include:

- What is the necessary condition for any commitment to be fulfilled?
- Commitments are only completed:
  - in some specific time
  - at some specific place
  - with appropriate resources (personnel, space, equipment, and money)

Managing Commitments

1. Determine time

2. Specify place

3. Identify the appropriate resources

Structures for Time Management

At this point in the lesson, students should begin to understand the benefits of managing commitments rather than managing time itself. Manipulating circumstances over which an individual has actual control allows students to create power in their working relationships, rather than passively waiting for time to control them.

Structures for Time Management

- Where is the last place you should put your commitments?
  - In your memory
- Why?
  - How many things can you keep in your memory?
  - What do you remember when you are upset?
  - How long does it take to get upset in your normal day?
- Need some structure outside of your memory in which commitments can exist

---

Commitment Management Exercise

- List ALL of the commitments you have for the next week (Look in all areas of your life)
  - What to track?
    - Tasks/appointments
    - Projects/themes
- Now put everything into a schedule with time/place/resources

---

Activity: Managing commitments

In this assignment, students practice putting commitments into time. The steps for this process are listed on the accompanying slide. This activity offers many benefits. First, it encourages students to start keeping a written record of their commitments, rather than relying on memory. Second, tracking commitments may encourage students to think carefully about what commitments they would like to turn down.

The accompanying slide is an Open Item List that requires students to write down their commitments (This chart is available in the Appendix of this book). Beyond simply listing their commitments, students also need to consider what resources they need in order to complete their tasks. Examples of the resources they may need include specific personnel resources, supplies (e.g., poster board and other materials) and someone to maintain accountability.

Open Item List

Date	What	Who	Resources	Date Due

Weekly Schedule

	Sun	Mon	Tue	Wed	Th	Fr	Sat
7AM							
9AM							
11AM							
1PM							
3PM							
5PM							
7PM							

After students have listed their personal, academic, and work obligations and activities, they can use the weekly schedule form to situate their commitments in time and place. The chart is available in the Appendix of this book.

The key aspect of this activity is to visually see what time is committed and whether in the course of the week it is possible to fulfill all obligations. Ask students to carry both forms around with them for one week and to refer to them repeatedly during the day. Suggest that they never accept new activities without writing them down.

If students really want to see how they are spending their time and what deters them from completing their obligations, have them do the following: At the end of the day, write down what was actually done (write this over what was scheduled). After one week students may see a pattern that identifies their actions.

Summary and wrap-up. Because of the nature of the managing commitments assignment, this material may be spread out over the course of multiple weeks. If the instructor wishes to spend more time on this subject, two possible extended topics are:

- Long-term planning (1-5 years out): What are you going to have finished in one year? Two years? Five years?
- Design your own commitment management system. Asking students to develop their own system ensures that they fully grasp the material, as well as improves the likelihood that they will continue to utilize a system in the future.

Teaching to the Learning Styles: Project Management

CONVERGERS

Creating a Gantt chart: This activity satisfies the Converger's preferences because it clearly identifies who is responsible for what activity and provides specific timing for when milestones must be completed.

Designing a tracking commitments system: Convergers will like this activity, because it allows them to integrate theory and practice, as well as develop a plan.

DIVERGERS

Listing project resources: Divergers should enjoy this activity because it allows them to be concerned with the individuals on the team and their satisfaction. Divergers generally are concerned that individuals have equal workloads and they do their best to help people perform within their comfort levels.

Brainstorming: Divergers will appreciate any type of brainstorming, for it allows them to widely consider potential solutions. It also allows them to be innovative.

ASSIMILATORS

Introducing learning objectives and project management terminology: These activities are attractive to the Assimilator's need to understand why something is being studied. Once Assimilators are shown the long term value of learning about project management, they will participate in learning the details of the material.

Formal lecture: The lecture components satisfy the Assimilator's interest in understanding the general principals for how something works. Providing the background theory ensures that they will be able to consider a subject in a comfortable forum.

ACCOMMODATORS

Project planning: Developing a WBS will appeal to the Accommodator's desire to accomplish something; however, this task may be completed too quickly to ensure quality.

Designing work breakdown structures: This activity is attractive to accommodators' concern for the organizing and planning processes. Identifying the project's goal and determining how to make it possible satisfies the Accommodators' drive to discover new ideas for themselves.

Class Adaptation Strategies:

A. *Size:* Large classes: Have students turn to their neighbors (two behind/two in front to create small groups for brainstorming exercises). Then have some share their responses with the overall group. Use teaching assistants as roving observers/supporters.

B. *Content:* The material from the 50-minute version should be tied to a specific project course. The personal time management aspects can be taught independently or tied to project management. If there is a team of five individuals, each with a schedule that is not written down and managed, then what chance is there to handle the complex, and unknown, components of a project? The instructor and the students should be challenged to design a project schedule that takes into account each individual's schedule.

C. *Classroom Culture:* Depending on the culture, the instructor might want to identify common assumptions regarding time management. If the students have very simple schedules without much variation then it is more likely that their scheduling details will remain committed to memory. However, students should be encouraged to develop systems that work with their own requirements, and that can be adapted as schedules become more complicated. To recognize the role that classroom culture may play throughout this module, the instructor might want to identify common assumptions regarding project management prior to beginning the lecture.

Follow-up Materials:

Project Planning Homework:

A. Reading assignment: Instructor choice (see instructor readings and references).

B. Homework (Project Management Planning): Have each project team submit a Gantt chart and responsibility matrix for their project. Review these to see if the team has a fair workload and realistic schedule.

C. Classroom follow-up 1: Have individual students create a Gantt chart for their specific project.

D. Classroom follow-up 2: After 2-3 weeks, have students review their Gantt Charts to see how their project is progressing, especially noting any changes in duration, responsibilities, and activities. Students should design a new Gantt chart illustrating how it differs from the first.

Time Management Homework:

A. Reading assignment: Instructor's choice (see instructor readings and references).

B. Homework (Time Management): For the week after the lecture on time management, students should complete the open item list and schedule. Instructor should remind them: Never do anything or say yes to anything without writing it down. The initial schedule should be written in pencil and then the final version of the day's events should be recorded in ink.

C. Writing assignment—Ask students to answer the following questions:
   • What did you observe about doing the exercise?
   • What did you observe about how your schedule changed? Where there typical interruptions?
   • Were you good at estimating the time it would take to complete your commitments?

D. Classroom follow-up: At the beginning of the next class ask for any observations about the commitment tracking exercise. Throughout the semester you can have them track their project's progress using the Gantt chart.

5.6 Project Management for Students: References

Van Aken, S. (2001). *University leadership development.* Blacksburg, VA: Virginia Tech.

Gido, J., & Clements, J.P. (1999). *Successful project management.* Cincinnati: South-Western College Publishing.

Weiss, J.W., & Wysocki, R.K. (1992). *5-phase project management: A practical planning and implementation guide.* Reading, MA: Addison Wesley.

Marmel, E. (2000). *Microsoft® Project 2000 Bible.* Foster City, CA: IDG Books Worldwide.

Smith, P.E. (2004). *Tools to improve the process of engineering design: An analysis of team configuration and project support.* Unpublished doctoral dissertation, Virginia Polytechnic Institute and State University, Blacksburg, VA.

Chapter 6 CONCLUSION

6.1 BESTEAMS Material

As even a rudimentary study of engineering course syllabi will show, assigning students to project teams as a means of accomplishing engineering project goals is not new. However, appreciation of the need to help students learn skills, tools, and techniques related to successful team performance is a relatively recent phenomenon. Indeed, external forces such as the industries that employ engineering graduates and accreditation demands via ABET have combined to make the teaching of teamwork to baccalaureate engineers an educational priority. The material in this book provides a first step in recognizing that student project teams will function more smoothly if undergraduates are taught basic teamwork principles related to the three key elements of successful teams:

- Personal Knowledge
- Interpersonal Effectiveness
- Project Management

The Personal Knowledge section addresses the human tendency to attempt to group or classify people and things that appear to possess similarities. The Kolb Learning Style Inventory (LSI) was chosen as the foundation of the module because it provides useful information for students about their own preferences in terms of learning new material. This information may be particularly timely for students early in their college careers, when these Introductory Modules are most likely to be used. In addition, the LSI provides a politically neutral lens for interpreting the differences found among team members. In a world that is ever more diverse, the need for this type of education is increasingly apparent. Understanding individual differences in terms of true abilities rather than stereotypical labels increases the likelihood that everyone's talents will be used to benefit both the team product and team process.

The Interpersonal Effectiveness module introduces basic information about how teams can be expected to function, namely by identifying predictable stages teams experience as well as ways in which teams can be coached through these phases. By understanding that some forms of conflict are expected, discomfort can be minimized for students. Likewise, giving and receiving feedback is another essential skill covered in this module. Introducing students to feedback processes also sets the stage for the appreciation of peer evaluation and review. The results of successful (or unsuccessful) feedback may be seen in the peer evaluations completed by the team. Faculty can link these two ideas, reinforcing the importance of both.

Of the three essential components of effective engineering project teams, the topic of Project Management is probably the most comfortable for engineers. The nature of most professional engineering projects requires these skills, which essentially define and codify the work so that multiple tasks can successfully come together at the appropriate times to ensure timely completion. What is unusual about the BESTEAMS model is introducing basic project management skills as early as the first year of the engineering curriculum. Most engineering programs reserve this type of material for specific upper level classes or even the master's degree. Since engineering students need less coaxing to appreciate project management skill training, many instructors begin with this topic and segue into personal knowledge and interpersonal effectiveness. Teaching younger students project management skills early in their college careers helps them on a personal level as well: the basic principles of breaking down a project into manageable pieces and committing to their completion are skills that can be translated to the lives of college students. Indeed, the extended time section of the Project

Management module introduces personal time management, thus leveraging this natural parallel between engineering projects and the project of being a successful engineering student.

6.2 Best Practices—Using the Modules

While the authors of this volume endorse these materials and have had success using them in the classroom, it is important to note that the modules were designed for maximum flexibility and adaptability. The PowerPoint® slides have been made available online so that instructors may either use them as offered or make changes appropriate to their particular class. The BESTEAMS version of the slides can be seen in this text while the electronic version is available for download and customization at **http://www.enme.umd.edu/labs/BESTEAMS/**

Faculty members are encouraged to remain open-minded to other changes that might be appropriate for their classes (refer to the Class Adaptation Strategies section in each MIP). For example, altering the sequence of the modules may be appropriate if students are assigned a large, complex project that requires immediate planning. Some instructors have presented all of the material in a half day training session prior to the start of classes (e.g., during engineering orientation). Others have realized that using the Interpersonal Module very early in the semester can function as an ice breaker allowing students to better get to know each other, which is an important step in successful team work. The modules are made to be used in the order and intensity preferred by the individual engineering instructor. The references provided at the end of each section suggest appropriate further reading to allow additional personalization of the lecture material.

The BESTEAMS teaching preference utilizes an interactive classroom where students practice the skills they have been taught. Subsequently, this material may challenge the instructor to acquire new material as well as adopt a different pedagogy. Conducting student centered activities, where students work together in ad hoc groups to complete the module exercises, require a shift in the thinking of the faculty member. Instead of being the "sage on the stage," the instructor becomes a "coach in the field." Faculty members interested in exploring what has been called problem based learning or collaborative learning should consult Felder (1998), who has applied the most relevant tenets of this educational material to the teaching of engineering. The research literature on the effectiveness of these learning approaches is strong. The BESTEAMS material within this book can provide both an incentive to help students become effective team members in the classroom and for engineering educators to develop their pedagogical talents.

While these goals may seem ambitious, modifications such as these are necessary for the continued vitality of the engineering profession. Although change can cause tension, this same stress can lead to innovation. Both ABET and the companies that employ engineering graduates have clearly spoken. Graduates of engineering programs must possess professional skills, including the ability to function on multidisciplinary teams, if they are going to be successful. It is incumbent on those who teach undergraduates to remember that the long term health of the field depends on their willingness to expand their comfort zone to include teaching process skills as well as traditional engineering content.

6.3 BESTEAMS Success

Do these modules work? At the time of this writing, BESTEAMS materials have been used by the BESTEAMS authors and partner faculty to train over 4000 students. Participant feedback has been overwhelmingly positive, indicating the vast need for teaching materials of this nature. Thanks to workshops held at annual conferences over the past four years, BESTEAMS leaders have experienced first hand the appreciation of faculty members for these flexible and easy-to-use team training modules. Comments such as the following were expressed: "I learned many new things and validated things I only tentatively knew." Likewise, workshop participants applauded the comprehensive nature of the BESTEAMS curriculum and its designers, noting that it was "great to have [a] psychologist involved." Today, BESTEAMS receives frequent requests for information, indicating that the modules are valued by an increasing number of instructors in engineering settings.

Students who participate in BESTEAMS training also have indicated an appreciation for the opportunity to expand their skill-sets. During 2001-2002, 1287 students from University of Maryland, Morgan State University, Howard University, and the United States Naval Academy were surveyed. Their responses illustrated the success of this curriculum. On a five-point Likert scale, responses to the statement "I enjoy working in teams" for all modules showed a mean above 4.0, where a 4 signaled agreement and a 5 signaled strong agreement.

Similarly, the mean for the statement "I understand the key concepts of today's workshop well enough to apply them in my team," was 3.91 for those trained with the Personal Knowledge module, 4.13 for Interpersonal Effectiveness, and an impressive 4.24 for Project Management. Most notable was the response to the statement "I have received formal training on teams in the past." Those trained in Personal Awareness had a mean of 2.96, Interpersonal Effectiveness was 3.12, and Project Management was 3.33, some of the lowest rated responses in the survey. These data clearly indicate the need for team training such as that offered by the BESTEAMS group. Students report both needing the information and that they enjoyed learning it.

For further discussion of these research results, and other BESTEAMS publications, see the website at **http://www.enme.umd.edu/labs/BESTEAMS/**

6.4 The Future of BESTEAMS

As noted in the Introduction, the BESTEAMS curriculum consists of three levels of material: Introductory, Intermediate, and Advanced. It is the intention of the authors to make the Intermediate and Advanced modules available to engineering educators in the future. For information on the status of this work, check the BESTEAMS website at **http://www.enme.umd.edu/labs/BESTEAMS/**

All of those involved with the BESTEAMS initiative are deeply committed to improving the teaching and learning of undergraduates in engineering programs. The authors will continue using teamwork as a vehicle for understanding all of the skills necessary for professional engineers, not just those that are technical in nature. While the pressures of external influences such as accreditation and industry tend to fluctuate from year-to-year, the satisfaction of coaching a student team through a challenging project-based learning experience remains.

6.5 Resources

Felder, R. M., & Silverman, L.K. (1988, April). Learning and teaching styles in engineering education. *Engineering Education, 78*(7), 674-681.

APPENDIX

TEAM FORMS

Team forms in this appendix also are available for download from
http://www.enme.umd.edu/labs/BESTEAMS/

Application Form for Team Membership

Name:_____   Major:_____

Academic Status: (check one)
    ____Freshman
    ____Transfer: Number of credits completed_____
    Previous Engineering Courses? _____
    Previous Math Courses?_____
    Previous Physics Courses? _____

Do you live on campus?____Yes   ____No

Do you have a car?   ____Yes   ____No

Do you have a job?   ___Yes   If yes, where?_____
                        ___No   If yes, now many hours per week do you work?_____

Do you have other responsibilities (extracurricular, family, etc.) that require a time commitment greater than 10 hours per week? ____Yes   ____No

How can you be contacted during the day (cell phone, parent number, etc.):
_____

Have you ever had the following experiences (check all those that apply)?

☐ Taken a metal, wood, or auto shop class (or have these construction skills)?
☐ Performed any car or bike repairs?
☐ Written a computer program?
☐ Created a web page?
☐ Have electronics hobby experience?
☐ Played a team sport?
☐ Coached individuals?
    ☐ Participated in an organized school club or activity?
    ☐ Used Excel or other spreadsheet software?
    ☐ Used Word or other word processing software
    ☐ Used PowerPoint or other presentation software?

Complete the following statements:
My **strengths** as a team member would include (e.g., previous experience on teams, construction, problem solving skills, etc.):

My **weaknesses** on an engineering project team might include (e.g., no previous team experience, preference to work alone, etc.):

Peer Evaluation Form

Your Name: _____   **Instructor Name:** _____

Student ID #: _____   **Course Number:** _____

Team Name: _____   **Section Number:** _____

Please fill out this form honestly, being as accurate as you can. Based on the rating scale below, circle one number in each box to indicate your perception of each team member's contribution to the team. Please provide an explanation for the scores you have given to yourself and your teammates on the reverse side of this sheet. Use an additional sheet of paper and attach it to this form if you need more room.

	Strongly Disagree		Neutral		Strongly Agree
	1	2	3	4	5

QUESTIONS	YOUR FULL NAME	A	B	C	D	E
		FULL Names of Teammates				
Regularly attends group meetings	1 2 3 4 5	1 2 3 4 5	1 2 3 4 5	1 2 3 4 5	1 2 3 4 5	1 2 3 4 5
Comes to meetings prepared	1 2 3 4 5	1 2 3 4 5	1 2 3 4 5	1 2 3 4 5	1 2 3 4 5	1 2 3 4 5
Asks for assistance when needed	1 2 3 4 5	1 2 3 4 5	1 2 3 4 5	1 2 3 4 5	1 2 3 4 5	1 2 3 4 5
Accepts responsibility for major tasks	1 2 3 4 5	1 2 3 4 5	1 2 3 4 5	1 2 3 4 5	1 2 3 4 5	1 2 3 4 5
Completes work in a timely manner	1 2 3 4 5	1 2 3 4 5	1 2 3 4 5	1 2 3 4 5	1 2 3 4 5	1 2 3 4 5
Identifies resources to aid team progress	1 2 3 4 5	1 2 3 4 5	1 2 3 4 5	1 2 3 4 5	1 2 3 4 5	1 2 3 4 5
Is respectful of others in meetings	1 2 3 4 5	1 2 3 4 5	1 2 3 4 5	1 2 3 4 5	1 2 3 4 5	1 2 3 4 5
Provides constructive feedback to teammates	1 2 3 4 5	1 2 3 4 5	1 2 3 4 5	1 2 3 4 5	1 2 3 4 5	1 2 3 4 5
Actively participates in group discussions	1 2 3 4 5	1 2 3 4 5	1 2 3 4 5	1 2 3 4 5	1 2 3 4 5	1 2 3 4 5
Sum Rating Scores:						

Include a brief justification for your rating of these items.

Team Evaluation Form

*Your Name:*_____

*ID Number:*_____

*Team Name:*_____

Circle the number that best represents your assessment of the team's effectiveness or performance in each category. Please use the following scale:

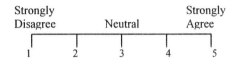

Question	Scale				
The team has a well defined set of goals and objectives.	1	2	3	4	5
All ideas are encouraged and fully explored.	1	2	3	4	5
Contributions of all team members are appropriately acknowledged.	1	2	3	4	5
Team members are able to resolve differences in a professional manner.	1	2	3	4	5
Team member assignments are given to maximize individual learning and mastery of new material.	1	2	3	4	5
The team meets deadlines and schedules.	1	2	3	4	5
Discussions are focused and useful.	1	2	3	4	5
Team meetings are always productive.	1	2	3	4	5
All team members contribute fully to team success.	1	2	3	4	5
Our team is highly productive; we exceed our expectations.	1	2	3	4	5

Use the space below and on the back of this form for any additional comments that you wish to make about the team

Giving and Receiving Feedback: Practice Exercises

A) Giving **positive** feedback about someone's behavior or attitude (3 students: one feedback recipient, one feedback giver, and one observer):

> You are a student in an Introduction to Engineering Class. You have been randomly assigned to a team to complete a group project. One of our teammates (Lin) has taken the initiative to write up a project final report incorporating the work of the rest of the team. The result is impressive. It is accurate and puts everyone's work together in such a way that the whole is greater than the sum of the parts. Please give this person feedback using the guidelines discussed in class.
>
> *Observer: Note the behaviors and words used by each student. What were the strengths and weaknesses of the interaction?*
>
> If time, switch roles and practice the scenario again.

B) Giving **negative (constructive)** feedback about someone's behavior attitude (3 students: one feedback recipient, one feedback giver, and one observer):

> You are a student in an Introduction to Engineering Class. Your team project has been going well, but one member has started to come late to meetings (something you all agreed would NOT happen when you set up your team ground rules). The situation is not out of control, but you can look ahead and see lots of work down the road where each team member will be needed. Please give the student negative, but constructive, feedback.
>
> *Observer: Note the behaviors and words used by each student. What were the strengths and weaknesses of the interaction?*
>
> If time, switch roles and practice the scenario again.

Open Item List

Date	What	Who	Resources	Due Date

Weekly Schedule

	Sunday	Monday	Tuesday	Wednesday	Thursday	Friday	Saturday
7AM							
9AM							
11AM							
1PM							
3PM							
5PM							
7PM							

INDEX

ABET, vii, 1, 3, 9, 45, 52, 101-102
Accommodator, 27, 34-35, 55
Adjourning, 8, 18, 47, 49, 57, 59
Advanced modules, vii, 4-5, 17, 103
Aimlessness, 19
Analogous estimating, 72
Assessment, iii, 7, 12, 25, 108
Assimilator, 26-27, 35, 55

Communication, 2-3, 5, 12-14, 21-22, 32, 38, 40, 44, 49, 55-57, 59, 61, 71
Conflict, 5, 7, 13, 16, 18, 20, 22, 36, 48, 65, 101
Confusing opinions with facts, 19
Converger, 26, 28, 35, 55

Dependencies, 73-74, 79, 82, 87-89
Dictatorial participants, 19
Disregarded ideas, 20
Diverger, 26, 28, 34-35, 55
Diversity awareness, 21
Duration, 72-73, 75, 82, 84-88, 98
Dysfunctional teams, 1, 6, 11, 18

Employment, 13
ENES 100, vii
Evaluation, iii, 4, 9, 14-17, 19, 38, 52, 58, 60, 68, 101
Expert judgment, 72

Felder, 3-5, 9, 44, 102-103
Feuding team members, 20
Football draft, 12
Forming, 8, 18, 38, 47-48, 50, 57-58

Gantt chart, 8, 72-74, 79, 82, 88-90, 98
GPA groupings, 12
Graduates, iii, vii, 1, 101-102
Group charter, 17, 58
Group work, 1, 49
Groupthink, 21, 23

Intermediate modules, 4-5, 72, 103
Interpersonal Effectiveness, vii, 52, 57, 64, 101
Introductory modules, vii, 2, 4-7, 14, 19, 31, 34, 47, 55, 64, 73, 78-79, 87, 101, 103

Kolb, 4-5, 7, 9, 25-28, 31, 33-34, 37, 40-41, 43-44, 47, 55, 63-64, 101

Learning Styles Inventory, 4, 25, 27-28, 31-34, 39, 43-44, 47, 55, 65, 101

Minority, 1, 7, 13, 21, 34, 35

Norming, 8, 18, 47-48, 57-58

Overbearing participants, 19

Peer evaluation, 14, 15, 17, 68, 101
Performing, 8, 18, 47, 49, 57-58
Personal Knowledge, vii, 25, 64, 101
Project Management, iii, vii-viii, 5, 8, 10, 62, 69, 71-73, 76-77, 79-81, 88, 90-91, 97-99, 101

Quantitatively based durations, 72

Random assignment, 13
Reserve time, 72
Resource loading, 86
Resume selection, 12
Rushing to conclusion, 19

Scholtes, 19, 23, 49-51, 53, 69
Secret ballot, 12
Skills
    process, 1, 3-5, 8, 11-16, 18-20, 25, 27, 37-38, 43, 47, 49-50, 52, 55-57, 59-60, 62, 64-65, 71, 73, 75-76, 81-84, 88, 93, 95, 99, 102
    product, iii, 3, 20-21, 28, 57, 62, 65, 82, 101
Skills Inventory, 12
Slackers, 6, 11-12, 16, 18
Storming, 8, 18, 22, 47-48, 57-58
Student learning, iii, viii, 6, 8, 11, 14, 25, 87

Tangents, 20
Team
    dynamics, 2, 5, 7, 14, 20, 32, 55, 63
    formation, 11-12, 18, 35, 39, 55, 57, 59
    grading, 6, 11, 14-15
    problems, 6, 19-20
    roles, 13, 15-16, 58
    project, vii-viii, 1-2, 4-5, 8, 11, 13-15, 17-18, 20, 33, 35, 38, 52, 56-57, 61, 79, 86, 90, 109

Teamwork, iii, vii, 1-3, 8-12, 18, 20, 28, 32-33, 35-36, 48, 56-58, 65, 69, 76, 101, 103
Tuckman, 47-49, 53

Underrepresented groups, 1, 6, 11, 21, 63
Unwilling participants, 19

Women, iii, 2, 6-7, 9-12, 21, 44-45
Work Breakdown Structure, 72-73, 79, 82-84, 86-87, 90